D1685787

CHRONICLES OF CONSENSUAL TIMES

Also available from Continuum:

Being and Event, Alain Badiou
Conditions, Alain Badiou
Infinite Thought, Alain Badiou
Logics of Worlds, Alain Badiou
Theoretical Writings, Alain Badiou
Theory of the Subject, Alain Badiou
Seeing the Invisible, Michel Henry
After Finitude, Quentin Meillassoux
Time for Revolution, Antonio Negri
Dissensus, Jacques Rancière
Politics of Aesthetics, Jacques Rancière
The Five Senses, Michel Serres
Art and Fear, Paul Virilio
Negative Horizon, Paul Virilio

Forthcoming:
Althusser's Lesson, Jacques Rancière
Mallarmé, Jacques Rancière

CHRONICLES OF CONSENSUAL TIMES

Jacques Rancière

Translated by Steven Corcoran

continuum

Continuum International Publishing Group

The Tower Building   80 Maiden Lane
11 York Road   Suite 704
London SE1 7NX   New York NY 10038

www.continuumbooks.com

Originally published in French as *Chroniques des temps consensuels* © Editions du
Seuil, 2005, Collection *La Librarie du XXle siècle*, sous la direction de Maurice
Olender

This English translation © Continuum, 2010

This work is published with the support of the French Ministry of Culture –
Centre National du Livre.

British Library Cataloguing-in-Publication Data
A catalogue record for this book is available from the British Library.

ISBN: 978-0-8264-4288-8

Library of Congress Cataloging-in-Publication Data
A catalog record for this book is available from the Library of Congress.

Typeset by Newgen Imaging Systems Pvt Ltd, Chennai, India
Printed and bound in Great Britain by the MPG Books Group

Contents

CONTENTS

Preface

The chronicles collected here are chosen from those I wrote over a 10-year period at the invitation of a large Brazilian daily newspaper, the *Folha de São Paulo*. The themes broached were sometimes proposed to me by the newspaper. More often, I was left to choose them from among the facts thrown up by what we call current affairs: national debates and worldwide conflicts, exhibitions or new films.

But the chronicle is not a way of responding to the events of passing time. For passing time, precisely, does not encounter events. Events are always ways of stopping time, of constructing the very temporality by which they can be identified as events. To speak of a chronicle is to speak of a type of reign: not the career of a king, but the scansion of a time and the tracing of a territory, a specific configuration of that which happens, a mode of perception of what is notable, a regime of interpretation of the old and the new, of the important and the ancillary, of the possible and the impossible.

I believed I could sum up what reigns today under the name of *consensus*. But consensus is not at all what is apt to be written about it by a disenchanted literature: a state of the world in which everyone converges in veritable worship of the little difference, in which strong passions and great ideals yield to the adjustments of narcissistic satisfactions. Twenty years ago, some minds, thinking themselves facetious, praised this new mood, sure to accord the institutions of democracy with its mores. Today, more minds, and often the same ones, thinking themselves solemn, condemn this reign of 'mass individualism' – in which they see the root of all dictatorships – for its enfeebling of the great collective virtues. We know common origin of these acts of bravery in the service of intellectual debates: they take from Tocqueville both his praise of the gentle mores of democracy and his condemnation of its inclination to servitude.

The pages that follow recall to us that consensus does not consist in the pacification of attitudes and bodies thus described. New forms of racism and ethnic cleansing, 'humanitarian' wars and 'wars against terror' are at the core of the consensual times chronicled here. Also featuring prominently are cinematographic fictions of total war and radical evil, and intellectual polemics over the interpretation of the Nazi genocide. Consensus is not peace. It is a map of war operations, a topography of the visible, the thinkable and the possible in which war and peace are lodged.

What consensus means, in effect, is not people's agreement amongst themselves but the matching of sense with sense: the accord made between a sensory regime of the presentation of things and a mode of interpretation of their meaning. The consensus governing us is a machine of power insofar as it is a machine of vision. It claims to observe merely that which we can all see in aligning two propositions about the state of the world: one maintains that we have come at last to live in times of peace; the other states the condition of that peace – the recognition that there is no more than what there is. All the arguments developed on behalf of the end of utopias and of history can be summed up in this nutshell. Allegedly, we had a time of war. This was the time when people wanted more than what there was: not simply economic groups but social classes, not simply a population but a people, not simply various different interests to align with one another but worlds in conflict, not simply a future to predict but a future to liberate. So, we now live in times of peace for having liberated ourselves of all these supplements, of all these phantoms, for realizing henceforth that what is, is all there is.

But all too often the peace invoked evades its obviousness: a body of workers rejects the assertion that there is only what there is, and that only governments know how to link what is to what will be; extremist parties renew the war against foreigners to the race; new wars inscribe rights of blood and soil on massacred bodies; terror and the war against terror take each other on. Consensus, therefore, is the machine of vision and interpretation that must ceaselessly set appearances right, put war and peace back in their place. Its principle aims to be simple. War, says the machine, takes place elsewhere and in the past: in countries that are still subjugated to the obscure law of blood and soil, in the archaic tensions of those who cling to yesterday's struggles and obsolete privileges. But because 'the elsewhere' avers that it is 'here' and the 'past' that it is 'today', the consensual machine must continuously redraw the borders between spaces and the ruptures of time.

Often bombs are required to divide spaces and confine 'archaic' wars to the margins of the consensual world. Time, as for it, is easier to manipulate. The consensus asserts a reality that is unique and incontrovertible, but only in order to multiply its uses, in order to bend it to the imperious scenarios of the present which leaves no room in which to dispute its presence, to scenarios of the past in which one confines the recalcitrant – the lame of modernity or survivors ill-cured of utopia – and of the future which commands the total deployment of energies. The chronicles gathered here strive to analyse the twists and turns accredited to time: continual diagnostics of the present and politics of amnesia, farewells to the past, commemorations, duties of remembrance, explanations of the reasons why the past refuses to go, repudiations of the futures which claimed to sing, exultations of the new century and of new utopias.

So, to analyse these consensual games, a chronicle must shift the sites of its investigation, venture to see other markings of time and invent its own temporal scenarios: for example, to compare the machines in Cronenberg's fictions or Matthew Barney's installations with those of Zola or Picabia; see, in present-day exhibitions, the Christly exultation of real presence confront a politics of the archive; discern the face given to the present in the new fictions of evil, historical or catastrophe films; or, the way that the legal debates on image-property rights are effacing the political status of the visible.

Even so, these chronicles do not claim to be providing an inventory of the signs of the times. This would remain within the logic of consensus, part its interpretative machine, which incessantly examines the times for its symptoms and looks into all the troubles of the social body, always recognizing in them the same evil: a want of adjustment to the present, a lack of adherence to the future. The consensus says that there is but a single reality whose signs must be depleted; that there is but a single space, while reserving the right to redraw its borders; that one unique time exists, while allowing itself to multiply its figures. All this goes to show that we are merely being asked to consent. The recent actuality of a referendum gave us the plainest illustration of this fact: even as it gave us the choice of voting yes or no, we were expected to say yes, or else avow ourselves as worshippers of nothingness. For the only oppositions that it recognizes are those of the present and the past, of affirmation and negation, of health and sickness. In this play of oppositions, the very possibility of a specific conflict necessarily disappears without remainder: one which bears on what there is, which lays claim to one present against another and affirms that the visible, thinkable and possible can be described in many ways. This other way has a name. It is called politics. The following chronicles attempt in their way to reopen its space.

CHAPTER ONE
The Head and the Stomach, *January 1996*

The people need something to believe in, the elites had said until recently. Today it is instead the elites who need something to believe in. Would our realist governors be able to accomplish their task had they not, from the Platonic utopia, retained at least one certitude: in the state as in the individual, the intelligent head must command the greedy and ignorant stomach? In Plato's time, the heads of philosophers were turned too far towards the skies and they occasionally fell in wells. The heads of our governors are firmly planted in front of the screens that announce the monthly indexes, the daily market reactions and the specialist outlooks for the short, middle and long terms. So they know very precisely what sacrifices the stomachs must make today for tomorrow and for the stomachs of tomorrow. They no longer need to convince the ignorant masses of the nebulous demands of the good or justice. They need only to show the people of the world of needs and desires exactly what it is that ciphered objective necessity dictates. This, in short, is the meaning of the word *consensus*. This word apparently exults the virtues of discussion and consultation that permit agreement between interested parties. A closer look reveals that the word means exactly the contrary: *consensus* means that the givens and solutions of problems simply require people to find that they leave no room for discussion, and that governments can foresee this finding which, being obvious, no longer even needs doing.

The French Prime Minister thus proceeded to announce to the population that from now on it would be necessary – in order to make up account deficits and balance retirement schemes – to forgo certain traditional social gains and that public service employees would have to work longer to get the right to retirement. Faced with a general public transport strike and the population's unwillingness to enthuse against these 'privi-leged' train and bus drivers, who made them walk in the middle of win-ter, the party of intelligence began to ponder. How can an obviously necessary reform be refused by the people of necessity? It must be, they concluded, that the reform was not well explained to them. They would have to work hard at it.

The affair is, all the same, strange. Because what do the authorities and the media do throughout the year, if not precisely explain to the popula-tion that nothing can be done except what our governments are already doing? How not to despair from the virtues of this pedagogy? The act of explaining is, in truth, every bit as strange as it seems simple. We, the governments, are, they say, too rational to be understood by the people, which is by no means rational. How, in fact, will the intelligent head ever make itself stupid enough to be understood by the unintelligent stom-ach? How can people, who do not understand by definition, be made to understand? Some thinkers of the elite found the recipe – again a Platonic one, in its own way: between the head and the stomach, there is the heart and, if the population were to be spoken to in the language of the heart . . . Unfortunately, there is no school by which to know what the heart could say clearly in these matters.

There is a further hypothesis, one that no serious government will ever admit, since it undermines the bases of its faith: if the explanation had no effect on the ignorant stomachs, then it is because they understood very well and do not think it convincing, in short, because they are not ignor-ant stomachs but intelligent heads. This hypothesis, ruinous for govern-ments, founds what there is real cause to call politics. Politics will continue to be confused by many people with the activity that it inces-santly counters – the art of governing. Politics is the way of concerning oneself with human affairs based on the mad presupposition that any-one is as intelligent as anyone else and that at least one more thing can always be done other than what is being done. Say our elites: all that was well and good in times of abundance. We can no longer afford the luxury of such extravagances. We shall learn with our thinking heads about the laws of necessity and shall have the stupid stomachs take note of this factual necessity.

This is the bottom of the matter. The thinking head of the Platonic legislator was reproached for being too far removed from the stomach to govern it usefully. The head of our governors suffers from the reverse misfortune: it is unable to distinguish itself from the stomach. Today's governing intelligence is but a knowledge of the automatism of the great global stomach of wealth. The opposition between the governors and the governed is turned into that between the ideal stomach and the vulgar empirical stomachs. This is perhaps the ultimate meaning of the word consensus: that the head which governs us is no more than an ideal stomach. The government used to say, in the old style, in the military style: there must be only one head. The watchword of our governments now is: there must be no more than a single stomach. Hence, the symbolic violence of conflicts such as the French strikes of winter 1995. Observers compared them to the victorious shows of force conducted by Ronald Reagan and Margaret Thatcher to break once and for all the power of workers' organizations. The governments here, in short, conduct a battle for the monopoly of the stomach, a battle to have it admitted that the system of needs has but one centre and a sole way of functioning.

Our elites promptly say that it is a matter of *make or break*, when confronted with the bad will of the people. However, there is very little bad needed for it to break. It suffices if the 'ignorant' simply realize one thing: that by identifying itself with the government of the stomach, the government of intelligence abandons intelligence's only recognized privilege – the right to attend to the future. It is in vain that our governments have their experts make long-term forecasts to justify the sacrifices that they ask for today. The mere announcement that the day's Stock Exchange is up and that 'the markets' have 'reacted positively' to these measures for the future suffices to instruct the 'ignorant', in bringing back that future to the daily activities of speculation. For the machine to jam, then, it is enough that the small stomachs to persist – as did the French transport workers in the defence of what the government calls their 'privileges'- and, step by step, the game gets turned around. The thinking heads then find themselves accused of being the mere organ of the great anonymous stomach of wealth, while the small greedy stomachs start speaking like intelligent beings and demand the right to attend to the future forgotten by our governors. Say the wise, these follies will be short-lived. Notwithstanding, from time to time it happens that societies suddenly relearn two or three unheard-of things: that intelligence is the best shared thing in the world and that inequality only exists by virtue of equality. These unheard-of things are simply what make politics meaningful.

CHAPTER TWO
Borges in Sarajevo, *March 1996*

In the introduction to his grand book *Les Mots et les Choses*,[1] Michel Foucault evokes the burlesque classification of a certain 'Chinese encyclopaedia' cited by Jorge Luis Borges, which divides animals into those 'belonging to the Emperor', 'embalmed', 'suckling pigs', 'who behave like madmen', 'who have just broken a pitcher' and similar sorts of categories. What strikes us, he maintained, before these lists which blur all our categories of the same and the other, is the pure and simple impossibility of thinking *that.*

Western reason has apparently made progress since. And the thinking political heads of the great powers recently brokered a peace agreement for ex-Yugoslavia giving *de facto* recognition of the division of Bosnia-Herzegovina into three ethnicities: Serbian ethnicity, Croatian ethnicity and Muslim ethnicity. The list is admittedly not as rich in imagination as that invented by Borges but it is no less aberrant. In what common genus could a philosopher teach us to distinguish between the Croatian species and the Muslim species? What ethnologist will ever tell us about the distinguishing traits of 'Muslim ethnicity'? We could imagine many variations of such a model. For example, the American nation divided into Christian ethnicity, feminine ethnicity, atheist ethnicity and immigrant ethnicity. People will say that this is no laughing matter. Of this I am utterly convinced. Hegel said that the great tragedies of world history were re-enacted as comedies. Here, conversely, it is farce that becomes tragedy. The Bosnian war is a military *coup de force* that not only caused a country to be torn apart, but that has also imposed as an 'objective given' of cold reason a way of employing the categories of the Same and the Other that makes our logic falter in an exemplary manner.

In classical terms, the Bosnian war was a war of annexation separately undertaken by two states, Serbia and Croatia, with the support of local irredentist populations, against another state, Bosnia-Herzegovina. Now, the chief endeavour of the aggressors was to impose, in lieu of this classic description, a new description of the situation: in its terms, an opposition, on the ground, between three ethnicities, whose identities, histories and cultures apparently prevented them from coexisting. The logical obstacle to this description was that there is no Bosnian ethnicity, and that Bosnia-Herznogovina is peopled with populations of diverse origins and religions who have coexisted for centuries, more or less well, as people often do under the sun. But we know, since Hegel, that death is dialectical, and the problem was resolved by the killing fields of ethnic cleansing. Killing the Other as Other is the surest way to constitute him in his identity, to impose on everyone and on himself the self-evidence of that identity. By systematically massacring Muslim populations in the conquered zones, the Serb aggressors proved by this act that they actually were an ethnicity. Of course, it is meaningless to talk of an 'ethnicity' defined by religious belief. But the problem is not to have criteria that make sense. They need merely exist in making coincide a specific difference and the tracing of a line on a map.

This coincidence, we know, is the same one to which a certain rationality also lays claim: the geopolitical rationality of the great powers. These great powers, while containing the territorial ambitions of the aggressors, also granted them their essential point: the 'rationality' of their principle of division in assigning each ethnicity its own territory. The big powers it seems were quite unconcerned by the contradictions that might arise between the great declarations of a supranational Europe and the ethnic gerrymandering of this small nook of that same Europe. But perhaps there is no contradiction. The logic of the great powers itself rests on a simple division. The great supranational spaces are for democracies. The countries of the former communist world will be able to enter it when, by their representative institutions and above all by their commercial development and budget control measures, they have proven themselves to be 'good students', ready to enter the great worldwide circulation of people and capital. As far as the rest of the world is concerned, so long as its state of development does not allow it to be able to afford the 'luxury' of democracy, it is better for it to be governed, as in times of old, according to the 'natural' criteria of birth, tribe and religion. In this logic, three territorialized ethnicities beat an indefinable and divided people. The unlocatable 'Muslim' ethnicity thus fits quite naturally into the most constant division of western reason, the same one that Borges' text plays with: whoever says 'Muslim' says 'Oriental', and the partition of Bosnia is a way of introducing into the heart of old Europe an ideal line of division. This line separates the world of western reason on the march towards a future of common rational prosperity and an 'oriental' world doomed, for an indefinite period, to languish in irrational classifications and the obscure identity laws of tribes, religion and poverty.

This symbolic geography, which places Japan in the west and Bosnia in the Orient, and this political imaginary, which increasingly identifies democratic universality with the global law of wealth, forgets, however, what happened a little east of Sarajevo 25 centuries ago. In this era, an Athenian called Clisthenes had his co-citizens adopt a strange reform. Until then Athens had been divided into territorial tribes dominated by local chefferies of aristocrats whose legendary antiquity obscured their power as landowners. Clisthenes replaced this natural division with an artificial one: henceforth each tribe would be constituted of separate territorial groups – a coastal, a city and an inland one – through the drawing of lots. These territorial circumscriptions were called *demes* in Greek and it was thus that Clisthenes invented democracy. Democracy is not simply the 'power of the people'. It is the power of a certain kind of people: a people deliberately 'invented' to dismiss simultaneously the old power of birth and the power that so naturally steps in to take its place – wealth. It is a people that affirms, beyond differences of birth, the simple contingency of the fact of being in such-and-such a place and not in another; a people that contrasts the dubious divisions of nature with abstract divisions of territory.

Democracy consists above all in the act of revoking the law of birth and that of wealth; in affirming the pure contingency whereby individuals and populations come to find themselves in this or that place; in the attempt to build a common world on the basis of that sole contingency. And that is exactly what was at stake in the Bosnian conflict: confronted both with the Serb and Croatian aggressors, and also with the claim of Bosnia's Muslim identity, Bosnian democrats strived to assert the principle of a unitary identity: a territory in which the common law would be the only principle of coexistence – the people as *demos*. In the facts, the other people triumphed: the people as *ethnos*, the people supposedly united by bonds of blood and ancestral law, however mythical. This triumph is not merely a local affair confined to a small end of Europe. No doubt we should remain level-headed about the prophecies announcing the widespread outbreak of ethnic, religious and other types of identity fundamentalism. Yet, so long as 'socialists' and 'liberals' act in concert to identify democratic government with the global law of wealth, partisans of ancestral law and of separating 'ethnicities' will be permitted to present themselves as the sole alternative to the power of wealth. And there will never be a shortage of appropriate classifications. For when it is forgotten that the first word of political reason is the recognition of the contingency of the political order, every absurdity proves rational.

CHAPTER THREE
Fin de Siècle and New Millennium, *May 1996*

We must 'let time take its time,' the late French President François Mitterand was fond of saying. Lionel Jospin, his luckless successor candidate, adopted as the first point of his programme to take France into the third millennium. No doubt sententious remarks about the time that we must wait for and the time that will not wait are part of the wisdom of nations and, consequently, of the rhetoric of our governments. But we can all well see the surplus value that the latter can extract from a *fin-de-siècle* that is also the close of a millennium. To say that we must 'let time take its time' amounts to placing oneself as the historical judge of the age of revolutions and communisms, in which the march of time was identified with the advent of a new era. This tells us, in short, that time is nothing other than time: the incompressible interval necessary for the sugar to melt and the grass to grow. Conversely, to take 1 January 2000 as the beginning of a new age, requiring all our thought and efforts in advance, is, on the contrary, to say to us that time is much more than time, that it is the inexhaustible power of production of the new and life, whose part we must play on pain of perishing.

These contrasting expressions of *fin de siècle* scepticism and new millenarism point to the strange mixture of realism and utopia that characterizes prevailing thinking. If we are to believe the discourse of the wise, our *fin de siècle* is the finally conquered age of realism. We have buried Marxism and swept aside all utopias. We have even buried the thing that made them possible: the belief that time carried a meaning and a promise. This is what is meant by the 'end of history', a theme that was all the rage a few years ago. The 'end of history' is the end of an era in which we believed in 'history', in time marching towards a goal, towards the manifestation of a truth or the accomplishment of an emancipation. Ends of centuries in general lend themselves to the task of burying the past. But ours injects a very specific touch of resentment into this epochal task. The thinkers who have made it their speciality to remind us without respite of all the century's horrors also explain to us relentlessly that they all stem from one fundamental crime. This crime is to have believed that history had a meaning and that it fell to the world's peoples to realize it. And even commemorations, of which our era is so fond, have assumed this necrological meaning. Not long ago they were designed to remind us of the meaning of our history, that is to say our debt towards the past and our obligation to accomplish its promise in the future. Today, their function has been inverted: their stake is to re-bury – or, at the very least, to set us at an exotic distance from – the time when we believed in history.

So, of course we no longer believe in promises. We have become realists. Or, in any case, our governments and our wise experts have become realists for us. They stick to 'the possible', which precisely does not offer a great deal of possibilities. This 'possible' is made of small things that progress slowly if they are handled with caution by those who know. We must no longer wait for the tomorrows that sing and for freedom to come and overturn oppression. We are implored simply to wait for the 'conjuncture' to be overcome. The good measure of realist time is not the present (we must learn how to wait). But neither is it the distant future. It is the time of conjuncture: we work for the following semester or the next year. And thus we measure, from one day to the next, the time that we must give to time so that, if all goes well, we will have one hundred thousand less unemployed the following year, or, if it doesn't, no more than a hundred thousand more.

But they do not get away with being realists so easily, and the modesty of the time that must be awaited suddenly reveals its other face: the franticness of time, which, as for it, does not wait. We can say that time needs time, but this will never be enough to see it yield its modest fruits. Time is not a leader of a liberal company, it is an old-fashioned monarch. It wants to be obeyed and loved before all else. It does not only want for us to follow its march. It wants us to go ahead of it, to give it in advance the gifts of our persons and our thoughts. Time's specificity is not only to be slow. It is never to stop. For their part, human beings have, we know, a distressing tendency to stop. As decades of workers' struggles have shown, people may want the future reign of work and to live in advance a future of infinite progress. This does not prevent, to the contrary, great care from being taken for the moment to separate clearly between leisure time and work time and strictly limit the latter to the advantage of the former. There is a way of living the future and another way of living the present. The utopias of new man and of glorious work sought in vain to redress this double appreciation of time, to prove that the present and the future, leisure and work were not different in their essence.

Our governments and our realist wise experts today take up the same song as the shamed utopians. By comparison with the latter, they promise us, it is true, very little. But for this little, they set the maximum condition. If, next year, we are to get an additional 0.2 per cent growth and a 2 per cent fall in unemployment, we have to mobilize full-time, we must stop clinging – like backward individuals – to the 'rigidities' of work time and its measure in salary terms, and put ourselves entirely at the disposition of time. We must become completely 'flexible'. This is not because time always needs us. But it can have need of us at any time. And we must be completely available, both for the moments when it needs us and for those when it doesn't. Time will yield us its modest fruits, on one condition: that we cease from stopping and from stopping it. In his theses *Über den Begriff der Geschichte*,[1] Walter Benjamin evokes the insurgents of the 1830 French revolution who showed symbolically their will to break with the course of time by firing gun shots at clocks. Our realist governments and entrepreneurs are utopians of another kind. They, too, would promptly break the clocks, but for another reason: because clocks sound the interruptions of time – the end of work, the closing of shops, the passage to recreation or from the history to the mathematics class . . . it is at this point that the sad economic reality is sublimated into the grand mystique of the new millennium. The future, to be built cautiously, step by step, becomes the Future which calls us and does not wait, the Future that we risk losing forever if we do not get a move on, if we do not ourselves rid of everything that keeps us from adopting its rhythm.

The *fin-de-siècle* managers of disenchanted realism then turn into prophets of the new millennium. They have preached submission to the law of the present and of the merely possible. They now exult the infinite deployment of our potentials for action and imagination. They ask us to cast 'old man' completely aside and muster up all the energies that will make us men of the future. Time, then, is no longer the support of a promise whose name would be history, progress or liberation. It is what takes the place of every promise. It is the truth and the life which must penetrate into our bodies and souls. This, in short, is the quintessence of futurological science. This science does not, in actual fact, teach us much about the future. Whoever reads its works to find out what shall be done in the future will generally be left wantinig. This is because its aim is different: it is not to teach us about the future, but to mould us as beings of the future. This is why school system reform always constitutes the core of the futurological promise. School is the mythical place where it is possible to fantasize about an adequacy between the process of individual maturation, the collective future of a society and the harmonious and uninterrupted progression of time. In the way of great indispensable mutations, Alvin Toffler once enlisted in a singular reform to the school system, which suggests that we dispense with the old routine of teaching blocks of literature, history or mathematics. From now on, it ought to teach the ages of life: childhood, adolescence, maturity and old age.[2] No longer was it a matter, in the old style, of a school system's preparing people for life. It was a matter of making these latter indiscernible with one another, in short of forming beings who are entirely of the times. Because the Time which is no longer susceptible to realize any utopia has itself become the last utopia. Because the realism which pretends to liberate us from utopia and its evil spells is itself still a utopia. It promises less, it's true. But it does not promise *otherwise.*

CHAPTER FOUR
Cold Racism, *July 1996*

At the heart of the supranational and liberal West, marching towards the absolute rationalization of social behaviours and the elimination of all ideological archaisms, racism is back. This march against time is something that might be wondered at. But political science is not philosophy. If, according to Aristotle, the latter begins with wonderment, the former's axiom is that nothing is ever surprising. And one of its favourite exercises is to demonstrate the utter predictability of the phenomenon that, moreover, it was powerless to foresee.

When it comes to racism and xenophobia, the explanation is always pre-prepared. These are phenomena, we are told, of backwardness. And phenomena of backwardness are the inevitable consequences of the march forwards. There is no economic modernity without a shaking up of traditional sectors of activity and a weakening the social strata linked to them. These worried populations, their futures threatened, thus develop regressive and archaic behaviours. They look for scapegoats and find them in 'others': foreigners who take workplaces, abound in the cities and receive all the considerations of the political class.

The origin of these schemas is easily recognizable; they are taken from old Marxist funds: when societies transform, the endangered petit bourgeois classes hold on tightly and enlist in the reactionary backlash. Moreover, we know that this type of Marxism has, practically everywhere, become the official ideology of liberal states and their intelligentsias. The reason for this apparent paradox is simple. There is one thing that liberal optimism is congenitally powerless to understand: the reason for which the march forwards can produce the march backwards. If there is one thing, by contrast, that Marxist literature brought to a point of impassable perfection, it is exactly this: the analysis of the historico-economico-sociological reasons for which history always gives rise to something other than that which it should.

The advantage of such explanations by means of sociological and economic conditions is that they always work, regardless of the said conditions. And they work for a simple reason, which is that, at the end of the day, they do no more than state a pure tautology, namely that the backward are backward. This tautology has, above all, the merit of assuring, without any need even to make it explicit, its incontestable converse, namely, that the advanced are advanced.

There are two things that the advanced seem to have a problem understanding. The first is that there is no need to be socially threatened or culturally 'handicapped' to resent the other as an obstacle to enjoyment and a threat to identity. In lieu of the specialists of political science, it was a psychoanalyst, Jacques Lacan, who announced, 20 years ago, the new racism to emerge within the very heart of a society that is completely occupied with endless enjoyment. The second is that, conversely, the pleasure in speaking and in reasoning is also shared by the so-called disempowered classes. If racist statements have always proliferated in company with the promises of unprecedented sexual performances – in the dilapidation of public toilets as well as in the modernity of internet networks – the reason is because they procure equal pleasure. And there is no need to suspect the combination of socio-economic misery and sexual misery. There is objective pleasure in playing with the formulations that serve to identify the traits of the other – as ridiculous, detestable or simply inferior. Above all, because there is pleasure in playing with words.

The theory of the advanced is that the backward only use words in weighing them down with a meaning which is that of their needs, passions, feats or frustrations. In the racist utterance, according to their argument, there will necessarily be a burden of popular or populist passions. In short, it will be necessary to believe in this utterance and to have great reasons for believing in it, if it is to function. The advanced seem not to perceive that the 'backward' are also daily the addressees of messages – political or publicity – that play on one or other of the two dominant registers of communication: expert explanation and derision. And the 'backward' follow very well. In one respect, racists speak like experts: they speak their language; they say less and less that Negroes are dirty or lazy; they explain more and more that there are economic constraints and thresholds of tolerance, and that, in the end, foreigners must be driven off, because if they are not, there is a risk of creating racism. In another respect, they know very well how to play on the undecidable status of reality and the status of ambiguous utterances which characterize the circulation of media messages. Today, there is practically no advertisement for a product that is not a play on words; barely any appeal to desire, or request to adhere to a belief, that does not pass via a suspicion or a derision, more or less pronounced, of the object of desire or of the very form of belief. It is not steadfast belief, rooted in lived experience, that makes us adhere to the order of our societies. On the contrary, it is word plays, suspicions of belief and the undecidability of opinion.

So, the racism developing today is not the fact of the 'backward of progress'. It is perfectly synchronous with the forms of legitimation of enlightened governments and advanced thinking. It reproduces the dominant forms of description of society and the prevailing mode of opinion, that of unbelieving belief, of belief that no longer needs to be believed to have an effect. Postmodern sociology, in agreement on this point with traditional Marxism as with government discourse, imagines that the deflation of belief is an impediment to collective passion and thereby assures social peace. But the deduction is false. Unbelief and suspicion can simply produce more intellectual, more ludic, more individualized, and, consequently, more effective passions, ones that are better adapted to the reign of sceptical adhesion and unbelieving belief.

A good example is provided by the growing excess of negationist arguments. The contribution that these arguments make is, in a sense, purely 'intellectual', conceived *in vitro*. The weapons of negationism were forged, without objective need or apparent passion, by university academics, who availed themselves of the favourite themes of advanced thinking: scepticism concerning the big words in need of deflation; rejection of globalizing interpretations and Manichean explanations. They declared that science had no taboos, that 'extermination' was a little bit too big a word, and that things needed to be examined in detail to see if they were proven and formed a single chain of causes and effects. And the reasons for the success of their arguments are simple: owing to the chosen object, they simply give a provocative form to the modes of thinking and the forms of belief germane to the dominant regime of opinion. If diverse parliaments have had to pass laws prohibiting people from denying the extermination, this is precisely because it was the sole solution by which to prohibit this exemplary transformation of the dominant modes of thinking into anti-Semitic provocation. It is because the daily bread and butter of advanced thinking is able, at any moment, to be translated into its 'backward' version.

'Enlightened classes, enlighten yourselves!' said Flaubert. This is the most difficult commandment to apply. Who will look for what he is assured of possessing? And why submit to examination theories that work in every case? Perhaps, quite simply, so that we no longer need to make them work.

CHAPTER FIVE
The Last Enemy, *November 1996*

The extraterrestrials are here. They've already struck. Los Angeles has disappeared in a deluge of fire. And upon interrogation as to what he wants on earth, the sole alien to be captured responds in virtually the only English he knows: death. On the morning of this July 4, as the United States celebrates its independence, the juvenile president addresses a circumstantial message to his troops: we are no longer fighting, he says in essence, for freedom and democracy as our ancestors did, we are fighting for our survival. The participants are overcome with enthusiasm at the idea of this new challenge, so much more exciting than the old, and which will be victoriously achieved through the exemplary cooperation between a white brain and two black arms.

This, we know, is an American fiction currently showing on cinema screens throughout the world by the name of *Independence Day*. And it might be wondered whether taking this declaration of political fiction seriously is worth the bother. Is the bombast placed on the fight for survival not simply part of the dose of shock stimuli that make up the cocktail of catastrophe films? The argument would be convincing precisely if the formula of the film did not appear slightly out-of-kilter. In this film, the visions of apocalypse and the special effects are, all in all, modest as compared with films of the same genre. What is striking, on the contrary, is the depiction of a tranquil America, where a president confronted with an extermination nevertheless strictly continues to share his parental duties as regards his daughter, and whose domestic virtues lead by their example to the regularization of free unions, the reconciliation of broken households and the rehabilitation of drunkards.

In short, the catastrophe scenario involves a strange discordance: on the one hand, it appeals to all the moral values in which a people likes to recognize itself, to the point of portraying the slightly outdated morality of a pilot who, having regularized his marital status, makes for a more effective combatant; on the other, it teaches us that in times of great threat, the common ideals of freedom and democracy associated with these private virtues can, as for them, be shelved in the antiquities store.

We can then question the relation between the moral virtue of good family fathers and a political virtue in which the fight against death completely supersede all democratic ideals. We recognize in it, of course, the persistence of a binary logic stripped of its other. Before the aliens, it was the landing of the Reds in Los Angeles or San Francisco that we awaited. In those times, the sureness of American victory was that of the victory of freedom and democracy over their mortal enemies. One fought, or one feigned to fight, to find out whether it was better to be 'red' or 'dead'. Since we no longer risk being red, the threat of death is all that remains, so the slogan of the supreme combat can be stated simply: better alive than dead.

The deduction is logical. Nevertheless, this fictional logic gives out a singular ring against the dominant tone of contemporary political science and historiography. These latter say that the collapse of the Soviet empire was the triumph of a democracy definitively reassured of its ideals in a world no longer subject to a division between two hostile blocs. Victory over the totalitarian enemy made the reign of democracy and the reign of peace identical. An entire present-day school of historiography identifies this end of our century's revolutionary cycle as the end of the long cycle of revolutionary democracy that began with the French Revolution. The revolutionary pretension to re-found radically the community is deemed to have tied democracy to the void of ideology and the violence of terror, for a period from which we have only just emerged. Today, at the other end of this long catastrophe, we are able to reconnect with the good tradition of democracy – that of the American Founding Fathers – that is, with the reasonable democracy – liberal and realist – which bases public peace on the exercise of private virtues and the enterprising spirit of individuals.

Now, this is the exemplary 'Americanness' that the discourse of the president-aviator shatters. It works to ruin the edifying identification of good government with the reign of peace, enterprise and liberty. Catastrophe films are not only fictions that restore, with little cost, emotions to populations that simultaneously want to enjoy the beneficial effects of democratic peace and to combat the ennui that it engenders. They remind us that the fictions of state cannot dispense so easily with the figure of the enemy, with the representation of an absolute threat. In one sense, the moral of the special-effect catastrophe film is no different to the one we are fed day after day by our reasonable governments: our societies must no longer be concerned with the fight for freedom and equality against their enemies, but with the struggle for survival, which is prey to the slightest blunder. The smallest wage rise, the smallest drop in interest rates, the slightest unforeseen market reaction is, in fact, enough to disrupt the acrobatic balance on which our societies rest and plunge the entire planet into chaos.

The invasion of extraterrestrial monsters who want nothing less than death is, in short, a grand spectacle that provides a face for the rampant fear that founds the legitimate exercise of governmental management. And it further illustrates for us one of the great founding myths of modern political philosophy: that threat of absolute war which demands each of us be alienated from our rights. In Hobbes' work, however, the threat of death comes from every man's being against the other. And, up until now, the enemy, and its threat of servitude or death, has always taken the face of another people, another political system. The America of Independence Day, as for it, is no longer threatened by any enemy other than death itself. By the same token, however, figuring this absolute enemy becomes problematic.

Another recent catastrophe film helps us to understand this. In *The Rock*, it is not from an army of extraterrestrials that the threat of chemical war being unleashed on San Francisco comes. It is from an American General, a former Gulf War hero, just like the president in *Independence Day*. The reason he takes the town hostage is that he wants to obtain indemnities for the families of the soldiers he has lost and America does not want to recognize. It is, in short, to gain recognition for the reality of death in real wars. This is precisely a right, however, that no longer has any currency. The wars that the Great Nation undertakes are mere police operations during which everyone is guaranteed a safe life. The only 'true' war is the total war against absolute Death. As a good patriot, the rebel general ends up recognizing this. He renounces the murderous enterprise destined to prove the empirical existence of death. He lets himself be killed to prove that death does not exist. All is well that ends well.

There is nevertheless a strange game being played here between death confronted and death denied, between absolute fear and the calm confidence jointly presented to us by the special effects of apocalypse films and the ordinary discourse of governments. According to Aristotle, tragedy has to purify the fear that it elicits, in order to transform troubles of identification into the pleasure of knowledge and contain passion within the play of theatrical space. We may ask what exactly is yielded by these apocalypse comedies with their fears, at once gigantic and so easily dissipated. We may ask what is gained from these promises to deliver us of empirical death at the price of a total mobilization against imaginary death. Do they not lead us to seek out imaginary culprits to blame for the threat that, promise or no promise, continues to weigh upon every life? This absolute other – the alien, death – which alone is authorized to give face to the enemy, is this not the one that, at the hour of the great proclaimed democratic peace, comes more prosaically stand in for this figure so close to the other: the representative of the other race, of the irreconcilable ethnicity or of the maleficent religion that imperils our identity and our survival?

CHAPTER SIX
The Grounded Plane, *January 1997*

Of a cinematographic oeuvre, as with any creative effort, there are two ways of speaking. The first is to judge it in accordance with its idea and to compare what the artisan has done with what he/she ought to have done or wanted to do. We thus begin with the fact that *Crash* is the filmic adaptation of a novel by J.G. Ballard, a sort of counter-utopia in the form of a pornographic science fiction novel, in which the automobile is placed at the centre of a Sadean scenario of pleasure founded on the infliction of destruction. We can further mention the interests of the director, David Cronenberg, in the great mythologies of our time, in mutant figures or man-machine hybridizations. And so we judge the film's images as the more or less adequate realization of the intentions of the one and the other.

And then there is the other way, based on what one knows nothing of or on the fact that we want some escapism, which involves placing ourselves before the thing, looking at the images and picturing the fable that their sequence proposes to us. We thus start off with what the film's first images show: a plane hanger. A young woman, apparently driven by an imperious desire, approaches a plane. She open her corsage, pulls out a breast from her bra, presses it ecstatically against the metal of the aircraft cabin and begins, with the machine, a body-to-body erotics that the soundtrack accompanies with the appropriate panting. Meanwhile, a man comes from behind to join in the party, and returns, in short, the young woman's machinic enjoyment to its human normality. At the film's end, we see the same young woman on the embankment of a highway, laying beside her overturned car, and ignoring her contusions to make love with her husband or privileged companion, who had amused himself by forcing her car off the road.

The film, in short, might be described as the story of an aviator who renounces flying. Her being in the hanger, then, had to do with her preparation for her pilot's licence, undoubtedly for the euphoria of cutting through the skies with the dream machine. But in the meanwhile, her companion initiates her into something that he himself has learnt: there is a totally other way to make love with machines and to use them for the fulfilment of one's desire. Preferable to the enjoyment of the beautiful plane cutting through the sky, is the car headlong on the encounter with another: the car which causes blood to flow, breaks the limbs, gashes the skin with scars, covers the body with prostheses but also, and above all, the car that one dents, smashes up, flips over, destroys, sets in flames.

So we might say that the point to which tale of *Crash* brings us is the latest episode, the finale of the great opera of the wedding of man and machine. Indeed, for the morale of this sulphurous film, which is given in its last image, could be considered the strict counterpart of another final image, a literary image that in fact marks this adventure's beginning. At the end of his *La bête humaine*,[1] after the conductor and his chauffeur have killed each other, ending a long tale of desires, jealousies and murderous folly, Emile Zola describes the deserted locomotive as it continues alone along its implacably straight line, driving, in spite of its crushed victims, humanity towards its future. The crime or the madness of its hero Jacques Lantier was perhaps to have preferred the enjoyment of the feminine flesh and of human blood to the faithful love of the machine. Then, conversely, in the 1920s, there emerged the great utopia of machines, which, harmonizing the aspirations of cinematographic art with the grand enterprise of constructing New Man, wanted to repeal the shamefulness of the 'bête humaine' in favour of a humanity that is in harmony with the faithful precision of the machine. 'In the face of the machine we are ashamed of man's inability', said Dziga Vertov, 'to control himself', in contrasting the 'unerring ways of electricity' to 'the disorderly haste of active people and the corrupting inertia of passive ones'.

The obstinacy of the heroes of *Crash*, not seeing in vehicles anything but machines by which to produce accidents for the purpose of procuring enjoyment, stages the revenge of man's disorderliness and corrupting feebleness. So, where some see a celebration of the futurist figure of man hybridized with the machine, I rather see the liquidation of the secular utopia of the couple of New Man and the dream machine. Ultimately, the film shows us that the only machine that can stay the course is the small human sexual machine, which turns metallic machines and their destruction to use, and which, in order to attain its goals, could do just as well without them by contenting itself – as the couple who've mastered the game shows us – to conjure them in words. In fact, all these scenes of horror and automobile orgasms might simply be stories that the couple tell each other in bed to add spice to their pleasure.

In this way, this film of futurist porno-fiction appears to present us a trendy and paradoxical version of the grand theme of the end of celestial ideologies and of the return to the simple and solid satisfactions that humanity gets into when it falls out of love with utopias. It is a humanist film in its way. And if we back up a century, we can also see in it the reversal of another scene: the scene of union between the absolute of liberty and the absolute of enjoyment procured by other's tortured body, illustrated by de Sade in the era of the French Revolution. Not so long ago, in an article titled 'Kant with Sade', Jacques Lacan endeavoured to show how the absoluteness of the Sadean imperative regarding the other's submission to my enjoyment was the hidden truth beneath the unconditionality of the Kantian law and moral imperative. Everything transpires as though the film inverts the demonstration. Let's look, for example, at the two female characters who go to the car park to make love in a car. They appear as though they have come to fulfil their duty: a duty fixed by the script, initially. The other heterosexual or homosexual combinations having already been exhausted, it is now their turn to have a go. This they do without apparent enthusiasm and without any obvious interest on behalf of the director, who cuts their frolics short. The reason for this is that the fictional duty is ultimately a moral one: an assertion of the equal right of every constitutable hetero- or homosexual couple to take enjoyment in association with the machine. The Sadean game of permutations has become a contract of generalized enjoyment and the violence on which it rested for de Sade is precisely situated in the relations of man and machine. Between partners a sort of pre-established harmony appears to prevail in which the enjoyment that one desires to obtain from the other seems, at each occasion, to be matched exactly by that which the other desires to obtain from me.

In refusing to have his film labelled pornographic, Cronenberg contrasts these sex scenes to the standard cinema tales of love and seduction, which he claims are fundamentally rape scenes. Love stories, we might answer, do in fact share a common feature with Sadean cruelty, which is that they are always based upon an inequality between two desires. The presupposition of the pornographic scene, by contrast, is that you do to the other what the other wants you to do. Pornography thus illustrates, in its own way, the liberal version of the social contract. This is why its visual empire develops along with the rhythm of development of consensual neo-liberalism. This is precisely what the final sequence gives us to see and hear: 'Are you alright?' asks the hero to his companion, whose car he has just pushed over the railing and who he finds again lying concussed on the side of the road underneath. 'I'm alright' she responds, which is to be understood not as an expression of her physical state but as an invitation, saying: 'you can go for it. I also desire what you desire'. In this way, all violence is reduced to the contract, and all the power of the machine to human desire. In the end, then, the film presents us with the counter-utopia of the *brave new world*, a rather fitting parable for prevailing notions about the 'end of utopias'.

CHAPTER SEVEN
Dialectic in the Dialectic, *August 1997*

How, today, are we to come to grips with Adorno's and Horkheimer's *Dialectik der Aufklärung*?[1] Its brilliance seems to have faded twice over: a first time, like that of a star of the constellation irremediably distanced in the past called Marxism; a second time, on the contrary, as the prototype, hackneyed by its copies, of the double discourse that is part of the banalized regime in which we live: the critique of the totalitarianism of Enlightenment reason that provides the liberal governmental order with its intellectual crowning point; and the critique of the culture industry that fuels the vaguely contestatory desires of intellectual opinion.

In one respect, in fact, this book seems to be part of the oft-attempted history of tearing Marxism, as a thinking of emancipation, away from the reason of the Enlightenment; away from a critique of the religion that sends religion earthbound after chasing it from the sky; away from a faith in science that reduces its spirit to a technical mastery of the world; and away from a progressist vision of history that subordinates the potential for emancipation to the necessities of the history of domination. Marxism, in one sense, is only the perpetually disrupted movement of that tearing away; it begins with the Marxian critique of the relations between human rights and the logic of capitalism. It continues via the recurrent polemic against evolutionist philosophy, which Adorno illustrates as much as Lenin or Benjamin or Gramsci. It is manifest once again in the 1960s with the Althusserian polemic against the twofold heritage of economism and juridical humanism.

And this interminable tearing away undeniably bears traces of the conflict between the philosophies of history within which Marxist theory and politics unfolded. The emancipatory confidence of the Enlightenment has perhaps only ever existed in the writings of Condorcet and a few others. And the Marxist identification between scientific theory and a practice of emancipation soon ran into a twofold denegation. On the one hand, Schopenhauerian pessimism, or the theories of decadence, inverted the assertions of progressivism, by accusing the rationalist pretension to worldwide mastery and human liberation of an original sin or illusion. On the other, scientism, with Spencer, Renan and many others, linked evolutionist philosophy to the theme of 'selection of the best' and the government of experts over the masses bound to servitude. The Nietzschean critique of civilization is situated at the exact intersection of these two traditions. And by the same token it entertains a complex relation to the Marxist critique of ideologies: it assists it in its effects only at the price of undermining its principles. And the consequences of this can be seen in the argument of the *Dialectik der Aufklärung*. What the latter proposes by way of a criticism of Marxist reason is a new version of the original sin of Greek rationality according to Nietzsche. In repudiating tragic wisdom, Socrates' fault becomes that of Ulysses' resisting the songs of the sirens. The fault, however, is the same and resides in the Apollonian hubris of the knowledge that wants to forget its Dionysiac side, the shadow-side that links it to the mythical world and the 'obscure forces of life'.

Adorno and Horkheimer, of course, link their denunciation of that original sin to the critique of social domination: their Ulysses does not simply guard himself against the Dionysiac songs of the Sirens. In plugging the sailors' ears, in obliging them to serve his own renunciation of enjoyment, he identifies the success of the common rational undertaking with the capitalist law of domination. He is therefore strictly opposed to Nietzsche's 'plebeian' Socrates. But this gap is made against the background of a common presupposition: that of a grand historical destiny of Western reason, construed as the accomplishment of an original sin. As such their critique of capitalist reason or of the culture industry thus appears much closer than it would like to the other great transformation of the Nietschzean primal scene, the one developed by the philosopher that Adorno riddles with his sarcasms; it appears as the leftist rejoinder to the Heideggerian critique of western metaphysics and its accomplishment in the technological domination of the world. There is, in short, a dialectic of the dialectic of reason. It strives to accomplish the interminable task of Marxist critique: to cut, at last, the umbilical cord linking the promises of revolutionary emancipation to the dangers of Enlightenment reason. It endeavours to contrast the perverted, instrumental and mediatizing reason of domination with an authentic reason, with a relation of intimacy between reason and the lived world which develops into a power of emancipation. But this breakthrough impels it towards another critique of the Enlightenment, a critique that casts the history of western reason and of its promise of emancipation as the irreversible development of a primary illusion.

This 'dialectic in the dialectic' founds the melancholic version of Marxist critique. But it also gives it an ambiguous destiny. Its critique of the cultural industry was then succeeded by the Situationist critique of the 'spectacle' – another grand, melancholic discourse on the uniform commodification of the world. Both have become commonplaces of that discourse of 'demystifiers' which accompanies each manifestation of the cultural industry – or of the 'society of the spectacle' – to such an extent that it becomes the latter's obligatory double [*doublure*] – the discourse of the 'clever' which this industry's 'stupidity' needs for its perpetuation. This dialectic enters into the strange destiny of what can be called post-Marxism. Declared dead with the collapse of the Soviet system, Marxism was, by the same token, liberated for all sorts of posthumous uses. On the one hand, official Marxism was called upon to do duty for neo-liberal politics, to which it lent the theory of economic necessity and that of the ineluctable direction of historical transformations; on the other, critical Marxism lent its disenchanted vision to those contestations of cultural commodities which accompany their development, while simultaneously maintaining reactive discourses which counterpose art's authenticity to the forms of its compromise with the calculations of state and the merchants of culture.

And, sure enough, the *Dialectic of Reason* denounces in advance any such use of its critique. It shows that art or the authentic culture that one claims to be upholding against the cultural industry stem from the same principle. The division between noble art and the cultural industry is heir to the first division symbolized by the gesture of Ulysses. In renouncing the enjoyment promised by the song of the Sirens, he reserves for himself the privilege of hearing only the song of promise and of peril that he has prohibited his sailors from enjoying. Civilized barbarism depends on this first exclusion. And here one feels the profound motif that separates Adorno and Horkheimer from the inanity of those weepers who periodically wallow about art's ruination in cultural commerce and politics. This profound motif goes further back than the Marxist critique of fetishism or denunciation of 'bourgeois' Enlightenment thought. Through the intermediary of Holderlinian poetry, it harks to that which is without a doubt the veritable founding text of the modern thought of emancipation, Friedrich von Schiller's *Über die ästhetische Erziehung des Menschen*.[2] To the established social division between the barbarism of the civilization of the Great and popular savagery, Schiller counterposes that chance at common humanity – at reconciliation in the sensory world – constituted by beauty. The resistant force of the *Dialektik der Aufklärung*, that force which separates its denunciation from all the contemporary commonplaces, lies in its refusal to yield on that fundamental aesthetic promise, on that horizon of a common sensible humanity. It also lies in the very radicalization of the theme of the promise. The romantic readers of Schiller made of art's beautiful totality the prefiguration of the free community. For Adorno and Horkheimer, on the contrary, art only perpetuates the promise at the price of breaking it, of inscribing in itself the sustained wound, the unresolved contradiction of every transfiguration of reality into a beautiful aesthetic appearance. This is the radicality which provides the denunciation of cultural banality with its force of anger. The problem is not that this banality brings art down to the level of the 'masses'. The problem is that it is a machine for satisfying all the needs, including 'elevated' ones, which deprives art of its force of deception, and therefore of its potential for emancipation.

This small difference is essential. We see simultaneously what weakens it. The fact is not that Adorno's and Horkheimer's Marxism is too tainted with utopianism. It is in fact missing the same thing that 'realist' forms of Marxism are missing: a *political* conception of emancipation.

CHAPTER EIGHT
Voyage to the Country of the Last Sociologists, *November 1997*

Tristes Tropiques[1] begins with a chapter titled: *La fin des voyages.* But why exactly have these travels ended and why is Brazil the privileged place for the verification of that end? These two questions presuppose another: what does it mean to travel if we are to understand by this not simply a displacement of bodies but an adventure of the mind?

To understand it, let us pause for a moment on a tale of travel through Brazil that is much older and much less polished than Lévi-Strauss'. In his *Mémoires d'un enfant de la Savoie,*[2] published by the author in Paris in 1844, Claude Genoux, former chimney sweep turned print worker, tells us of his years of errancy and in particular of his voyage to Brazil in 1832. He set out for it by chance, he tells us. A letter lying about in the Marseille port informed him that Brazilian barbers were in need of leeches. So he bought a big lot of them and transported them to the other side of the Atlantic. With his leeches sold, various circumstances detained him in the country and he relates to us the most extraordinary. The main characters are a caiman that devours his travelling companion, a boa constrictor that threatens to devour him, and a black slave by the name of Papagaïl – the former king of an African tribe who revolts against the injustice of the *fazendero,* massacres his master's entire family and is hanged. For Genoux this last episode provides the occasion for an intense mediation on the contradiction of a country in which public opinion and a liberal press coexist with the barbarism of slavery and corporal punishment.

Genoux's tale presents us with the classical figures of the travel story. What we discover, to start with, is that the other country really does resemble its otherness, that the story describes precisely the animal and human menagerie and vegetal props recognizable by those who have never been there and never will. The tropical adventures that Genoux recounts could have been invented even if he'd never left Europe. And one indeed begins to suspect that perhaps he did not actually ever leave. The principle of the equivalence whereby caimans, boas and parrots lend support to their own figuration is in itself simple: the map of the world only ever presents the traveller with the stages of humanity's development. The territory of Brazil is a map of time. The America/Africa encounter arbitrated by the European is one of humanity's past with its future. Before the painted canvass of the tropical forest, the young Savoyard and the old king-become-slave communicate in the language of the universal spirit. And this language is easily reducible to that strange literary language which only exists in school texts and the prose of autodidacts: 'White man, you are the first of your colour who has lowered himself or rather who has shown himself to be big enough to lower himself to help a poor Negro. – Can I treat the colour that heaven gave you as a crime? – Never, I think, was such a discourse pronounced by a White Man in the presence of a Black Man . . . '

In identifying himself with the language of the universal mind, this literary language, which no one has ever spoken, annuls the scepticism that the traveller draws from his experience. He traces the line of a future at the end of which the New World will end up precisely being identified with the territory of a new humanity which has accomplished its march towards civilization and that will find itself governed by an *order* which will be the recapitulation of its *progress*. This hope of a community governed by the law of an ordered past was, in Genoux's time, the object of a young science which Auguste Comte formulated and Émile Durkheim taught to the masters of Lévi-Strauss. This science, which is more than a science, consists in the idea of a society that transforms its science into beliefs and common rituals; it is called sociology. Travelling to Brazil means travelling to the country of sociology.

This is the voyage that the Brazilian journey of *Tristes Tropiques* brings to its end. The tracing back of the time which goes from Paris to Sao Paulo and from Sao Paulo to the Rondon line is the path by which sociology's meaning is inverted. This is the 'sadness' of the Tropics. In disembarking at Santos, Lévi-Strauss would have surely been aware of the famous phrase of a French president: 'Brazil will always be a land of the future'. And he, too, could also have described, without leaving Paris, the tropical avenues and villas of Rio – similar in setting to the seaside stations of 1860s France – the herds of cattle grazing in mid-Sao Paolo, the new and instantly aged buildings, or the decadent aristocracy of the racetracks and the Automobile Club. It is this tropical décor that takes the place of Genoux's caiman and boas. The future of civilization is already no more than the imitation of its past. But a serious consequence follows from this: if Brazil's future is in the past, the same holds for the future of sociology.

This is shown already in the 'sociological minuet' carried out by the chosen society which surrounded the young French professors of Sao Paulo University, and in which each sociological species is represented by a unique specimen: the communist and the catholic, the racing dog amateur and the amateur modern painter, the local erudite and the surrealist poet. What is this miniaturized social world, if not the caricature of the sociological principle of an organic society constituted by well-differentiated functions? The great sociological faith from which the theory of progress drew a second wind, namely that which was to give a soul to the new reasonable republics, is made to look by the Brazilian mirror suspiciously as if it is only a game of society.

And yet, sociology is not an illusion. But to encounter it one must move towards the real territories of those Indians who, according to the master of Lévi-Strauss, peopled the working class areas of Sao Paolo and, according to his Paulist interlocutors, had long since disappeared from the Brazilian soil. On the shore of the Rio Paraguay or near the Rondon line, the ethnologist at last finds sociology in act. The Caduveo's face painting or the topography of the Bororo village carry out the same intellectual programme: to invent a cultural order which imposes its norms on nature. For these 'savages' are 'greater sociologists than even Durkheim or Comte'. They feel just as much repugnance for that which associates the pleasures of sex with the vulgarity of procreation as taste for that painting which imposes the geometrical regularity of its decors on the 'natural' traits of the face.

But the solution to this intellectual problem is also the solution to a political one: the complex structure of the Bororo village and the dividing up of sides in the face painting of the Caduveos integrates into a same structure the two contradictory elements of their social organization: equality, expressed in symmetry, and the asymmetrical distribution of three hierarchized classes. Sociology was born in nineteenth-century Europe for precisely this end: to collapse into a single structure the hierarchy necessary to the life of the social body and the equality claimed by the man of democratic times; to make this structure the principle of a faith and a ritual by which the members of a society manifest, in a half-conscious half-unconscious way, the principle of their social cohesion. Far from exoticism, the funerary ritual of the Bororo realizes the ideal of the positivist Republic, namely that which inspired the commemorations of the Third French Republic.

So Brazil really is the land of sociology. Only, it is among those populations in the process of final extermination, repressed to the furthest depths of its territory. The ethnologists complicity with the 'savages' vision of the world, then, is more than a character trait or a principle of method. It is a solidarity with the last authentic servants of sociology. The slow death of the Nambikwara is not only the last episode of 'civilizing' conquest. With them will die not so much the last savages as the last true sociologists. And this Nambikwara leader who seizes a simulacrum of writing, conceived uniquely as a means of power, anticipates the death of this last true sociology. He makes of it a simulacra similar to the 'sociological minuet' of the Paulist elite.

That is the final lesson of the Brazilian voyage, that is of the ethnologist's return to the sociological continent. However, the Nambikwara is not the last people to be visited by the author of *Tristes Tropiques*. Departing from scientific method, he seized the occasion to enjoy a stay of ethnological truancy among the Tupi-Kawahib. There, he said, he was really able to play Robinson Crusoe and enter into a relation with the savages, which the absence of an interpreter left in its mute virginity. Return of ethnological science to the good Rousseauist savage? Or discovery that the serious sociological science was no less utopian than the reverie of the good savage?

CHAPTER NINE
Justice in the Past, *April 1998*

For 6 months, official France seems to have been occupied by a single event: the trial of Maurice Papon, former functionary of the French state of Marshall Pétain, for his complicity, between 1942 and 1944, in the arrest of Jewish men, women and children gone missing in the death camps. This trial could have resulted in a simple confrontation. On one side, relatives of the deported were demanding reparations for the crimes perpetrated against their kin. On the other, stood a functionary who had fulfilled his role as functionary of the collaborationist state without inner concerns or an excess of zeal. He signed the arrest and deportation warrants that fell under his authority, without worrying personally either about organizing the search for Jews or about finding out the fate of the deported. A sentence of 10 years in prison was handed down to sanction his undeniable and clearly demarcated responsibility.

However, this is where the simplicity of things starts to get fuzzy. What is the relation of commensurability between the 10 years in prison imposed, 55 years after the facts, on a man now 87 years of age and the martyrdom of those who were assassinated *en masse* in the death camps? And why did a trial that could not result in any verdict proportional to the wrongdoings of an individual involved in a mass crime take on such an importance?

This lack of proportion shows, first of all, the singular function that the instance of the judiciary has today. Every political matter of rights or wrong, of justice or of injustice, takes the form of a trial conducted in a real or imaginary court of law. At the same time that the French were daily informed of the Papon trial's unfolding, they could behold, in all bookstore windows, the *Livre noir du communisme*,[1] which featured an advertising sleeve announcing: *85 million dead*. Some have questioned the figures: how are we to count the victims of the Chinese famines and must they be counted as victims of communism for the same reasons as those who were shot or who died in the camps? But this is not the heart of the problem. The function of figures is more legal than statistical. From Volin[2] to Solzhenitsyn there has been no lack of people to disclose the crimes of communist regimes. But they did so in another political mode. They testified as victims of communism, denouncing it in the name of another political idea, whether anarchism, the 'veritable' communism or the restoration of the old monarchic and religious order. Today something else is at stake: the number of deaths is identified with a court of history whose decision has been made, that has delivered a verdict no longer on a regime but on an ideology, that is, ultimately, on a time when one believed in ideologies. The court of history, in sum, has settled the account between the present and another time: that of Volin and of Solzhenitsyn as much as of Lenin or Stalin – in short, the time of politics.

It could be said, in the same way, that the Papon trial involves a settling of accounts between the French people and the French Vichy state and its participation in the Nazi undertaking of extermination. The trial of an individual thereby also becomes the trial of the past. It gets identified with a court of history, charged with stating a truth that would simultaneously permit a statement of collective guilt and relegate this guilt to the past, at last drawing a line between this past and us. The 10 years of prison meted out to a functionary of the French state declares, once and for all, the guilt of that state as such. This sentence simultaneously marks the distance which for us makes it a pure object of judgement. But this equivalence is indeed misleading. To transform the trial of a functionary into the trial of his state is a contradictory thing: it is to accuse him at once for what he did as a functionary of this state, which is guilty as a whole, and for what he did not do, as an individual – disobey the state whose functionary he was.

A functionary, by definition, serves the state. Maurice Papon served the collaborationist state. After this he served the Republic of General de Gaulle. The state abhors a void and the Gaullist Republic took servants of state from wherever it could find them: from among the servants of the 'French state' that had simply served the state in general, without an excess of militant zeal. Thereupon, Maurice Papon became an exemplary servant of the French Republic, notably directing the repression of an Algerian demonstration in October 1961 during which nearly two hundred demonstrators were beaten to death and thrown into the Seine.

This latter state crime was not implicated in the trial. If it was nonetheless referred to during proceedings, it was in the framework of this significant syllogism: since he committed this crime of our Republican state, which nobody dreams of prosecuting, he may well have committed the other crime of the collaborationist state. The fact that he has always been a good state servant proves his general inability not to serve the state, hence his implication in the crime of the state he served in 1942.

Ought we to believe that the trial brought against Papon is the trial of the state in general and of those who cannot bring themselves to disobey it? And has the court of history, in imposing 10 years of prison, decided in favour of the 'right to disobedience' whose legitimacy is the cross of political philosophers? This would have been quite strange, if we bear in mind what happened at a Parisian airport on the very same day as the verdict: some passengers on flight from Paris to Bamako refused to take it together with clandestine workers that the French Interior Ministry was forcibly sending back to their country. The Minister announced immediately his intention to prosecute these recalcitrant passengers for 'obstruction to the circulation of aircraft'.

It is therefore quite unlikely that the court's verdict aimed at enshrining the right to disobey. The conviction of the overly faithful state servant refers instead to the obligation to disobey in the past: not only in the repressive context of the Vichy state, but in a time when there was sense to obeying or disobeying. It says to us that back in those times, to obey or to disobey was a decision for individuals. It sets us, in sum, back in the ambiance of the existentialist epoch. In those times, Sartre could state the sentence that once elicited so much scandal and scorn: 'Never have we been freer than under the German occupation'. It was a time of commitment and responsibility: one in which each would choose 'for all' and was 'responsible for everything in front of everyone'. The conjunction between the court's conviction (in the past) and the Interior Ministry's threats (in the present) relegates this time to its place in the past. Today, to obey or disobey the state is no longer a problem. Not only because the state is legitimate, but more profoundly because it claims no longer to want anything, to be no more than the humble executor of an impersonal necessity. What sense would there be in disobeying a state that does not command anything and only obeys the circulation of flows? In Plato's times, the sophist Antiphon contrasted the justice of nature to that of the law according to the following simple principle: one who infringes upon the law shall be punished only if seen. However, one who goes against nature will be subjected to punishment every time. This is the logic that our states have readopted for themselves: they tell us that their regulations simply conform to the natural laws of the equilibrated circulation of wealth and populations. The travellers on that day who did not want to go to Bamako were made guilty, in relation to the French state, of a rebellion that is neither more nor less than an 'obstruction to the circulation of aircraft'.

This is how the settling of accounts with the past proceeds. Disobedience has had its day: namely the time when individuals stood in opposition to the wills of other individuals or of states, the time of politics and of ideologies. The justice system salutes this time and lets us know that it is past. In some ways, the verdict of the Papon trial is a farewell tribute to existentialism.

CHAPTER TEN
The Crisis of Art or a Crisis of Thought?
July 1998

Among the debates of opinion in which 'thinking France' is obliged to be interested, the crisis of art figures prominently. The intellectual magazines whose vocation it is to raise the tone of debates about the great problems of society rarely miss a chance to take stock of the crisis in question. Some years ago, *Esprit,* an organ of Christiano-social hermeneutic liberalism, launched a polemic against the 'anything goes' attitude that today, with the complicity of the functionaries of culture, is invading museums and galleries. *Le Débat,* an organ of hard-line liberalism, recently presented a three-way match up: Jean Clare, a detractor of the avant-garde in his *La Responsibilité de l'artiste,* went head to head with Philippe Dagen, whose book titled *La Haine de l'art,* attacks the detractors of contemporary art. Yves Michaud, author of *La Crise de l'art contemporaine,* as for him, refused to get involved in this debate between two people by translating the 'crisis' in terms of a sociological evolution in which mass democracy and multiculturalism liquidate not exactly art but the utopias of art. While from the left-wing daily newspaper *Libération* to the far right-wing journal *Krisis,* Jean Baudrillard repeats interminably the refrain of art's fatal nullity in a world where all is image.

It cannot be assumed that this show of polemics enlightens the reader much about the following questions: in what does the crisis of art consist? And above all, what exactly is the name of art being used to refer to? Significant in this respect are the names of the stigmatized artists. Around the star couple Joseph Beuys/Andy Warhol, these attacks aim at the set of currents which, from Pop Art to conceptual art and demonstrations by Fluxus at the Dokumenta exhibition in Kassel, have likened their practice with a specific contestation or repudiation of the traditional forms of art. The crisis of art is, in a word, the new name of what, 30 years ago, was called contestatory art – or the contestation of art. But, then, if they were completely logical, the denigrators of the crisis should rather rejoice to observe the withdrawal or the banalization of such forms which – what's more – involve only a very limited sector of the vast domain of arts, at the border separating the plastic arts and the performing arts.

But perhaps the rhetoric of denunciation is more important than what it denounces. And more than to any considerations of the present forms of music or cinema, dance or photography, the current critique of 'art in crisis' adheres to a pre-constituted ideological logic. Its argumentation, in fact, is only a way of cashing in – a propos of art – on the same arguments that fuelled the denunciation of the 'master thinkers' in the 1970s and that, since the 1980s, have interminably fed the denunciation of *la pensée 68* and calls to restore healthy philosophy, Kantian morality and republican politics. Nothing is more significant from this viewpoint than a read of *La Responsibilité de l'artist.* Its author, Jean Clair, has attained renown for some brilliant essays, memorable exhibitions, and his role as the director of the *Musée Picasso* in Paris. Of his incontestable knowledge of painting, however, there is nothing to be found in this writing which, in the footsteps of the Glucksmanns, Finkielkrauts, Ferrys and other oracles of the intellectual French right-wing, accuses the inevitable scapegoat. This, of course, is German Romanticism, blamed as much for art's contemporary decadence as for all the crimes of Nazism and Stalinism. German Romanticism is held responsible for diverting art's modernity via the frenzied avant-garde search for the new and its forced anticipation of the future. It absolutized the notion of art and subjected it to the irrational fantasies of the 'originary'. Art's bankruptcy, therefore, has accompanied the crimes of utopia, both being born in the same soil. Yesterday, Jean Clair tells us, German expressionists – the heirs of Romanticism via Symbolism – even paved the way for Nazism (which would condemn them) by blurring the boundary between meanings and the meaning. Today this will to art, henceforth devoid of all content, only continues to proclaim itself by means of the 'anything goes' attitude to which it gives itself.

Here, once more, the conclusion to be drawn is not obvious. It could in fact be said that today this utopia has come to term. The 'anything goes' attitude so decried would spell the end of the dictatorship of the avant-gardes and open onto the peaceful coexistence specific to the forms of a postmodern art and a multicultural society. This is, roughly speaking, the argument developed in Yves Michaud's book. But this multicultural happy ending hardly appeals to the big names of the new French ideology. For them, it is not the simple multicultural consensus that must be counterposed to the bankruptcy of utopias, but the renewed meaning of republican and national values. So, in a timely fashion, the final combat between the enlightened Kantian cosmopolitans against the dark Herdian ages of the soil and the origin comes to be relayed through another combat: that opposing the natal charms of the French republican country to the American multicultural desert. The bankruptcy of contemporary French art consists, then, in its submission to the aesthetic diktats of post-war America. As such, Jean Clair traces the triumph of the 'all-over' abstractions of American expressionism to its self-evident cause: the infinite similitude of the flat American landscape, a gigantic suburb uniformly cut through by straight highways. In opposition to this highway desert stands the charming bocages and sunken lanes of the French countryside of which those writers from Normand country, Maupassant and Flaubert, are the painters.

If the truth is to be told, there actually are a few mountains in the United States (a colloquium was even organized by a Montana University a few years back hoping to make Jean Baudrillard notice this detail). Nor do French highways meander through wheat fields any more than their American cousins. And Flaubert, for his part, hated that France of the bocages, preferring above all else the emptiness of the deserts of the East. But the ideology of resentment has its reasons, and cares as little about the reality of facts as the coherence of its argumentation.

There is, however, a logic to the operation that transforms the writer in the 'ivory tower' into the loving painter of his village. There is, in effect, a singular fact that characterizes all the discourses about the crisis or end of art. All together, they only speak, under the name of art, of painting or of that which has taken its place. Jean Clair, who dramatizes the artist's responsibility, would have no doubt found more convincing arguments for so doing in the works of writers, musicians and directors than in painting, whose powers of mass mobilization are far from obvious. Neither does Yves Michaud, who de-dramatizes the crisis of art, seem to think that art extends beyond museums and galleries. Yet, cinema and dance gladly boast of their good health. Contemporary music is tending to leave its ghetto and encounter other forms of music. And even when they engender ennui, rare are those who accuse contemporary composers of neglecting their work. Nobody speaks of a 'crisis of literature' even if few living writers provoke wild enthusiasm. Why, then, consider that art in general is in crisis, if upon entering the gallery to see paintings, one instead finds piles of old clothes, stacks of television sets or pigs cut in half? And even if it were possible to tax the totality of contemporary painting with being null and void, why would the momentary eclipse of one art among others spell the final catastrophe of art?

The reason is, Jean Clair tells us, the painted image has a power that cannot be achieved by any other aesthetic genre. Why exactly? Because 'painting' in these discourses designates everything other than an art: it is a sort of ontological revelation or primary mystique. Painting here is conceived as an originary sacrament of the visible in which divinity or Being appears in its glory. 'I do not look at the canvass as a thing', said Merleau-Ponty, 'my gaze wanders in it as in the aureole of Being'. The painter's all-consuming vision, according to him, opens onto a 'texture of Being' that the 'eye inhabits as man does his house'. We understand easily enough that the eye does not discover this house of man which is also the dwelling of god in Damien Hirst's dissected animals. There is a whole swathe of the mystique of the 'visible' that is fuelled by this phenomenological version of the Christian transubstantiation. And, at the end of the road, the post-Situationist critique of the 'spectacular' comes, in Baudrillard, to communion in that nostalgia of lost presence and concealed incarnation. The accusation levelled against the 'Romantic divinization' of art itself requires this religion of the visible to which it gives the name of painting. Art goes as it can. But the thinking of the soothsayers, as for it, is not going very well.

CHAPTER ELEVEN
Is Cinema to Blame? *March 1999*

The release of Roberto Beningi's film *La vita è bella*[1] re-ignited the conflict over what cinema – and more generally art – can and cannot show of the Nazi extermination. The film's fictional given – a Jewish father who manages to have his son believe that their forced stay in a camp is a game – clearly mimics, in troubling fashion, the negationist argument according to which facts can always be interpreted differently. It also rekindled the polemic of those who maintain that the horror of the extermination cannot be represented. And that assertion about unrepresentability in turn provoked the reaction of those who refuse the censorship thereby placed on the image. Among the latter, Jean-Luc Godard proclaimed recently that no one has the right 'to prevent people from filming', at the risk of drawing suspicion to himself. In an article in the Parisian daily *Le Monde*, Gérard Wajcman, a psychoanalyst and author of a work with the telling title *Objet du Siècle*, inquired into the cult of the image underlying that claim and reasserted the position illustrated by the works and statements of Claude Lanzmann: no image can be adequate to the horror of the extermination.[2] For the image always trivializes the extreme and gives a human face to crime.

Beneath its apparent clarity, the debate's formulation raises many questions and leaves many unclarities. An expression by Adorno, uttered too quickly and glossed for too long, declared art impossible after Auschwitz. We see today how this culpabilizing of art in relation to horror can be interpreted in two different ways. According to Lanzmann, cinema is guilty when it tries to provide images of the Shoah and thus participates in trivializing it. According to Godard, it is guilty of not having filmed these images, of having ignored the camps, neglecting to seek out its images, and of failing to recognize that, in its own fictions, it had announced the work of death. According to the former, cinema fails in the consideration of horror because of the image; according to the latter, it fails for not having had images of it. Clearly, these two contradictory versions of guilt involve two different ideas of the relation between art and the image, two ideas of art which are based, in the last resort, on two theologies of the image.

We can surely grant Gérard Wajcman that Godard's position stems from something entirely different than a defence of the right to the freedom of images. It stems from a conception of cinema that is properly speaking iconic, which Godard illustrates at length in *Histoire(s) du cinema.* In the latter, Godard says that cinema is neither an art nor a technique; it is a mystery. This 'mystery' is nothing other than the incarnation. Cinema is not an art of fiction, the cinematographic image is not a copy, not a simulacrum. It is the imprint of the true, similar to the image of Christ on Veronica's Veil. The image is an attestation of truth because it is the very mark of a presence. Because there were camps, there were images of it. Cinema was guilty for lacking them. And those who want to proscribe the images of the horror simultaneously refuse testimony of it. This argument can be read the other way around: there must be images of the camps so that the truth of the image can be attested and the art of cinematography devoted to its worship.

All the same, is the condemnation of this cult of the image entirely clear? It asserts the unity of an aesthetic viewpoint: whoever wants to make images of the unrepresentable horror will be punished for it by the aesthetic mediocrity of the product. But what exactly does it mean to 'make images'? Both Lanzmann and Benigni, in *Shoah* and *La vita è bella*, respectively, make moving images. What differs is the function of these images, the end that they pursue and the way in which the filmmaker arranges them to ordain them to that end. Lanzmann intends to attest the reality of a process on the basis of the very programmed disappearance of its traces. The image, then, cannot reproduce what has disappeared. It must do something else, indeed two things simultaneously: both show the effacing of the traces and give the floor to witnesses and historians to reconstitute with words the logic of the disappearance accomplished on the ground – show the logic of the extermination and of its concealment. To this end, in subordinating images to the words which make them speak, Lanzmann rediscovers the paradox stated by Burke more than two centuries ago when he contrasted the powers of poetry to those of painting: words are always more appropriate than images for translating all grandeur – sublimity or horror – which exceeds the measure. More appropriate, precisely, because they spare us from having to *see* what they *describe*. To 'show' the horror of the final journey towards death, the analysis of the marching orders and the cold explanation of the workings of the 'group discounts' granted by the *Reichsbahn* will always be superior to a re-enactment of the 'human herd' being led to the abattoir, for two reasons that are only contradictory in appearance: because they give us a more exact representation of the *machine* of death, by leaving us with less to see and picture of the suffering of its victims.

In short, Lanzmann's intention demands a certain type of art, a certain type of 'fiction', that is to say of organization of words and images. Of course, Benigni's intention is totally different. With regard to the extermination, he is not concerned to testify to or to negate anything. He takes it as a situation suitable for bringing the constitutive logic of his character to its point of paroxysm. The whole film is in fact constructed around a sole given: the ability of one character to perform a permanent miracle and to transfigure every reality. He is just as incapable of denying the reality of the camps as he is of saying anything about them. The film's mediocrity stems not from the supposed ethical indignity involved in fictionalizing Nazi horror and having us laugh at it. It stems from the fact that Benigni has not fictionalized anything at all. An author-actor like Benigni, Chaplin, in his *The Great Dictator,* took the risk and won the gamble of making us laugh at Hitler. But in order to make a fiction about Hitler's person, he paid the highest price: he consented to break the unity of the Tramp form, to play the inverse roles of the dictator and of his victim and to cast them aside to speak in his own name. He thereby stages the *displacement* of his character onto the *Führer's* podium. The director Benigni, as for him, is unable to invent the displacement of Benigni the actor. Unable to make a fiction of anything, able only to repeat *ad infinitum* the gesticulation of the illusionist. His camp scenes are not bad because they give images of something that cannot or must not be put in images. They are bad because they have neither more nor less reason to be than the preceding ones.

The question therefore bears on the fictional capacity of the *mise-en-scène* and not on the dignity or indignity of the image. Nor does it bear on what the image in itself can or cannot do. If posed in terms of effective-ness, the argument of 'trivialization' by the image is indeed ambiguous. Since the attestation of the exceptional event runs a twofold risk. To sub-tract it, in the name of its exceptionality, from the ordinary conditions of representation of events is as dangerous as making it commonplace by representing it according to the same rules as all others. We must then think that the enemies and devotees of the image alike have some other stake in the matter. In criticizing the salvational value that Godard, *qua* disciple of Saint Paul, accords to the image, Gérard Wajcman maintains that he does not intend to put into play another theology of the image, namely the Mosaic prohibition of representation. But if it is hardly the sacredness of the law that is at stake here, the sacredness of something else – art – may well be. The argument of the unrepresentable aims to shore up an equivalence between art's modern destiny and an historical mission. According to this logic, Malevitch's *White Square on a White Back-ground*, in ruining the principle of figuration, allegedly gives to modern art its true subject: absence. To prove the image's truth, Godard had to see in the camp of the *Great Dictator*, or in the rabbit hunt or dance of the dead in *La Règle du jeu*,[3] the prophecies of the extermination to come. To attest to art's mission, its critique must put the same logic to work, that is to see in the anti-representative manifestos of the 1910s modern art's prophetic anticipation of its vocation: to account for the 'object of the century' – the extermination. In this way, a theology of artistic modernity contrasts with a theology of the salvational image. It is not sure that this combat serves justice to what films – good or bad – really do.

CHAPTER TWELVE

The Nameless War, *May 1999*

'The Gulf War will not have taken place', was the prediction, in early 1991, of a French intellectual.[1] According to him, the military machine of deterrence henceforth obeyed the general law of a world in which reality cedes place to simulation. In the matter of war, as in every other, the logic of power was to simulate events to prevent them from happening. A 'real' war could not happen because it would contradict the deterrent exercise of military power. The empirical events seemed to contradict that beautiful deduction. The reasoner hastened to show that this was not at all so: the Gulf war, he made clear, could not take place. And, in fact, it *has not taken place*. In effect, its operations were only decided upon by computer calculations and its effects transmitted to us by television screens. Between a computer screen and a television screen, the only space in which events in general and war in particular can take up room is a screen-like space, the space of virtual reality. That which could not take place did not take place except on the screens of simulation.

To assert that non being cannot *be* has always been the favourite pastime of sophists. However, we must not be so hasty as to impute this kind of reasoning to the irrepressible propensity of intellectuals to deny reality for the love of words. Intellectuals are more observant and more realistic than is claimed. They know that words are not the opposite of reality. Words are, on the contrary, what give reality its consistency. If the sophists have so many facilities today by which to declare the non-being of no matter what reality, this is in fact because the artisans of that 'reality', unable to give a name to what it is that they do, have abandoned it to them. It is not the fault of computers and the virtual. Today no one courts the risk of saying that the Kosovo war will not, is not, or has not taken place. And yet, who can give a name to the military operations undertaken by NATO? Intervention in a war? But what sort of war? Hardly a foreign war: the allied powers do not recognize Kosovo as an actual nation under attack from another. So, is it a civil war? But then who could have given the allied nations a mandate to intervene in the internal affairs, as violent as they may have been, of another nation? We are left with a third type of war in which the opposed terms are not two nations or two parts of a nation, but humanity and anti-humanity.

That exact schema was the one retained: the intervention pressed forth to save humanity, in the figure of the Albanian Kosovars, victims of a genocidal undertaking, against the perpetrators of this genocide: the anti-humanity embodied in a bloodthirsty dictator. Between humanity and anti-humanity there are no territorial borders, scarcely a limit to the right to interference. But the contradiction is evicted from the principle of war only to be radicalized in its conduct. The war conducted in the name of a humanity to save is a total war by definition, a war entirely determined by its objectives of making the rights of a humanity respected, and which does not recognize any limitation as regards the means of ensuring that respect. How then to conceive of a restrained humanitarian war? A war in which selective bombings are designed to bring the anti-humanitarian criminal to the negotiating table, while leaving the terrain free for his troops' operation of massive liquidation of the people representative of humanity whose rights had been impinged upon? It all happened as if the humanitarian war divided itself into two sets of operations, situated upstream and downstream of the territory that was abandoned to the undertaking of ethnic purification: on the one hand, military operations that aim at once to deter and to punish the doer of the crime; on the other, humanitarian operations to welcome hundreds of thousands of victims of this crime.

These apparent contradictions have led some to suspect the existence of obscure goals or secret activities, hidden behind the humanitarian parade. But it could be that there is no contradiction, that there is a convergence, more profound and more troubling than any concealed dealings, between the logic of ethnic purification and that of humanitarian war. The principle behind both of them is one and the same: the negation of politics. Ethnicism revokes the very space of politics in identifying the people with the race and the territory of exercise of citizenship with the ancestral soil. Ethnic purification does not simply consist in driving an undesirable ethnicity from a territory. It consists in constituting it as an undifferentiated herd, simultaneously denying the collective reality of a people endowed with a public life and the singularity of the individuals comprising it. Humanitarian war claims to oppose the respect of human rights to this process of twofold elimination. But the 'human' that it defends has very specific characteristics. The figure that it takes is precisely the product of the enterprise of cleansing, the figure of the victim. Here lies the core of this strange configuration – the humanitarian: which endlessly proliferates in those *no man's lands* that spread out between the politics that is no more and the war that is no war. Previously it was said that war is the continuation of politics by other means. The humanitarian war is the continuation of the elimination of politics.

There are two forms of elimination of politics. There is the identification of the government of the people with the self-regulation of populations through the automatisms of the distribution of wealth. That is the painless elimination of politics; it is called consensus, and is practiced wherever wealth permits it. And there is the type of elimination within reach of the poor, the violent elimination that identifies the government of the people with the law of blood, soil and ancestors. The 'humanitarian' is, then, the twofold system, military and assistential, by which the consensus of the rich contains the excess of the war of the poor. The defeated peoples, the individuals denied – all are treated by the humanitarian regime as though they were constituted by ethnicism – as victims, as masses. The Kosovars or the Bosnians – and the Serbs, too – are also individuals as singular and as different from one another as we claim to be, are the participants of an intellectual and artistic life capable of just as much sophistication as ours, and are the actors of a public life marked by as many antagonisms, but the humanitarian regime is not bothered about this one bit. Ethnic purification, the dissuasive war and humanitarian assistance all share a common logic of massification.

This logic was illustrated by the 'blunders' leading to the deaths of Serb travellers and Albanian refugees, both confused with military targets. Seen from planes and computers, indeed, the ones and the others are distinguishable with difficulty. But the problem does not concern the relations of the real and the virtual. It concerns the relation between two humanities, between two ways of perceiving and counting – by individuals or by masses. The aerial-strike war is a war that states it will not risk the lives of those waging it. That no American soldier's life is put in danger is the implicit contract which supposedly makes the American war in the Balkans acceptable for the American people. The respect of this contract from the side on which the bombs are launched can provoke disappointment on the side on which they are received. But the point is that the count is not the same: the life of an American military member and those of 20 civilians, Serbs or Albanians, do not compare. The humanitarian war that the 'democracies' – as our states are called – are conducting in the Balkans is a war at the frontier of two humanities: a humanity of individuals and a humanity of masses. To fight for the humanity of the Albanians of Kosovo against the inhumanity of the Serbian cleansers is tantamount to separating these two humanities. And, from this point of view, the sometimes blind logic of the bombings aims true: from the sky of western individuals, the masses of Milosevic's soldiers and the streams of refugees can be confused. Attackers and the attacked are on the same (bad) side of the border: in the terrestrial world of archaic mobs to which is opposed the celestial world – modern, rich and democratic – of populations of individuals. If NATO's aerial war is not one, the reason is that it does not refrain from denying what every war supposes: the existence of a terrain shared by both parties.

This is why the blunders committed in relation to ill-identified targets scarcely prevent people's adhesion to this non-war war. In effect, they confirm the imaginary geography that sustains it. According to this logic, the redoubtable bombs are by no means the ones that American aviators drop. They are the ones that explode, so to speak, in their backs, on the territory from which they themselves come. One day, the images of the Kosovo victims disappeared from the screens of CNN. Their place was taken by other torn-apart bodies, other teary-eyed women and children, victims of the home-made arsenal perfected by two Colorado schoolboys. Two ordinary young Americans shot into the pool of American lives, constituted them as a same herd of victims, in the name of an apolitical 'Hitlerism', likened to a certain sensibility, a specific way of dressing, of affirming one's individual difference and the identity of one's small group. And that sufficed to blow up the imaginary geography of war proper, to annihilate the border traced by the other bombs between a world of individuals and a world of mobs. The murderous madness of

CHRONICLES OF CONSENSUAL TIMES

Eric Harris and Dylan Klebold brutally recalled the following fact: that between the tastes which singularize the individuals of advanced societies and the passions and suffering of mobs attributed to archaic ethnicities, no proper war, nor any level of GDP, traces any border. This is only done perhaps by that thing which has become enigmatic and which is called politics.

CHAPTER THIRTEEN
One Image Right Can Sweep Away Another,
October 1999

The polemics, which recently erupted in France, between the Ministry of Justice and the corporation of photographers over 'image rights', does not only concern relations between the rights of journalists to inform through images and the rights of individuals to have their own images and private lives respected. It is the strangeness of the actual state of the relations between images, the law, politics and even art which has here found itself placed under a revealing light.

The conflict arises from two dispositions of the bill relative to the presumption of innocence and the rights of victims. The first prohibits the publishing of victims wearing handcuffs, the second the publishing of photos of crime victims in situations that undermine their dignity. Both are part of the same overall perspective of developing the rights of persons: protection of private life, of the image and of the dignity of persons, the presumption of innocence of all persons so long as they have not been recognized as guilty. Even the 'accused' has had a name change. Henceforth is he 'indicted'. A step further was taken with the proscription of every material image of the indicted's incarceration. But this extra step has troubling consequences. The point was not simply to euphemize the name of a factual state. At stake was to make its materiality invisible. The protection of the private person tends to become a suspension of the very visibility of the event. What cannot be judged is not to be shown, must not have any visibility. This implicit rule conceals another behind it: that the only judgement is henceforth that delivered by the courts. Previously, the image of the guilty party functioned as an appeal to a judgement of public opinion, independent of that of the judges, even as a challenge to the latter. The image is part of the classic political combat that puts into question the legitimacy of existing laws. In France, once again, one of the leaders of actions undertaken by farmers against the McDonalds chain recently waved his handcuffs about in front of the eyes of journalists as an emblem of the justice of his struggle. With the new logic of the presumption of innocence that is a right of every private person, what is annulled is the political dispute over this gap between two forms of justice and two forms of judgement emblematized by the figures of the innocent culprit and imprisoned righter of wrongs.

The protection of the person and his/her image thus produces an operation that is indissolubly political and ontological. It tends to subtract, along with a certain type of judgement and of political judgement, a part of the visible. This part is not that of the contagious example or the unbearable horror that were once proscribed. On the subject of violence, indecency or horror, hardly a thing is censored from our screens. The part proscribed is the undecided, litigious part, the one that fuelled political conflict, by putting into question, along with the 'guilt' of the agent, the nature of the act itself. The question is thus to know where this subtraction stops, if it does not spread, along with the visibility of facts, to the very attestation of their existence.

This question is the one raised by the second prohibition, that of showing the victims of crimes in situations that are harmful to their dignity. Hence, the widow of a prefect assassinated by Corsican terrorists was enraged by a photo showing her husband with his head lying on the ground. A similar scandal emerged surrounding the image of a woman bared by the blast of a terrorist explosion in the Parisian metro. But these singular cases in which a person's call to have their dignity respected bring forth with them the immense chain of photos which have made us see and continue to make us see the horrors that have stamped our century. Confronted with legislators, journalists and photographers have brandished these past testimonies of history, including photos from Nazi camp survivors or of the small, naked Vietnamese girl burnt by napalm as well as those that still today register the daily harvests of mass crime in Bosnia or Rwanda, in Timor or in Kosovo. To be sure, the appearance of victims does not conform to the ideal of human dignity. Simple good sense responds that it is the situation that is essentially undignified and this is precisely what the image aims to testify to.

But the affair – which is both political and ontological – goes further than the simple opposition between the respect for victims and the duty to inform us about their situation. The reason being that at stake is not simply to know if we will or will not be able to disclose, to the doctors and righters of wrongs, the suffering and injustices of the world. Photography attests to two things simultaneously: it attests not merely to the fact of the crime, but also to its nature, in marking the weight of the presence and common humanity of those who the exterminators treat as subhuman vermin. What genocides and ethnic cleansings deny is in fact a primary 'right to the image', prior to any individuals' ownership of his/her image: the right to be included in the image of common humanity. Ethnic cleansing or extermination is always the demonstration-in-act of its own presupposition: that the exterminated do not belong to that from which they are excluded, do not really belong to humanity, not, in any case, to that which has the right to exist in that position and in that place. This is why ethnic cleansing or extermination finds its logical accomplishment in the getting rid of traces and in negationist discourse.

Does evoking, against these photographs, the harmed dignity of victims not replace the first denied right – the right to bear an image of common humanity – with a right that these victims don't need: the right of ownership of one's image that is exercised only by those who have the means to exploit it? It might be said that this is only a question of the school. It is hardly hoped that Kosovar victims will front up for indemnities for the publishing of their pictures in the French press. The minister then responded to the dismayed by affirming that the bill does not concern the facts of war. This 'reassuring' response is baffling. For it refers the image to a division of domains and of genres that is indeed in question. From his point of view, Hitler was not waging war against the Jewish people, he was eliminating unhealthy parasites. Similarly, the Serbian militia were not waging war against the Kosovar people. They were eliminating those who were not in 'their' place. And the 'humanitarian' operations that respond to ethnic cleansing are not claiming to be intervening in a war. If the fact of the extermination and negationist discourse have taken on their well-known importance in contemporary discourse, it is because they themselves also testify to the present-day uncertainty surrounding the lines of division between these spheres: the public and the private, the political, the police and war. The right of the proprietor and the right of the victim illustrate in a nutshell the tendencial blackout of the political world, to the advantage of a twofold scene: on the one side, the private global scene of private interests; on the other, the scene of ethnic clashes and humanitarian intervention.

But it is not only the image in general – and the photographic image in particular – that is caught in this torment. A specific idea of artistic modernity is implicated in it as well. The double success – political and artistic – of the photographer in our century consists in his/her exemplifying the privileged link that modern art had to the image of the anonymous – those anonymous people who, in the nineteenth century, appropriated this image, which had always been reserved for the privileged, to those who had a name and made history. The objective of the great reporters who bore testimony to the century's horrors was related to that of the Doisneaus and the Cartier Bresson's in their surprising of street kids or of anonymous lovers. Both expressed a time when anyone at all was likely to be a subject of history and an object of art. It is this 'anonym', the common subject of democratic politics and modern art, which will also see its image effaced, split into two. As the law extends its ambiguous protection to the presumed innocent and to the dignity of victims, the anonymous of the photographic legend front up to ask agencies for the commercial price of their image. In a world divided into owners of images and owners of dignity, not only politics but also art is having its images compromised.

CHAPTER FOURTEEN
The Syllogism of Corruption, *October 2000*

'All corrupt' used to be the shout when news would emerge of the fraudulent dealings of such and such a politician. But in our day, everything tends to get sophisticated and treated in the second or third degree. When the president of the United States of America has to explain, with a red square on the screen, the details of his relationship with his secretary, or when the former treasurer of the French president's party censures the bribery and corruption that prevailed at the Paris Town Hall as the same president was its mayor, no longer are demonstrators to be seen in the streets of the corresponding capitals, gathering together to inveigh against their rotten leaders. Instead, we hear consternation coming from solemn-sounding men, themselves often current or former politicians. What do these revelations serve to do, they say, if not to give the enemies of republican governments the chance to shout 'all rotten!'? It is politics, they say again, that these people are assassinating. Who will still want to govern in the face of the relentlessness of judges and the media? The 'republic of judges' and its 'media lynching' discourage the good will of those who take up the burden of public life. And they discredit politics itself. It is really high time to throw a veil over all these turpitudes and restore politics to its nobility.

These *pro domo* pleas clearly lend to suspicion. But, besides the politicians, who have a few too many interests in the affair, there are the philosophers, disinterested by definition, with their smatterings of Aristotle and the common good, of Lock and civil government, of Kant and the Enlightenment, and of Hannah Arendt and the glory of public life.

France produces an incredible quantity of them, and a good many circulate between the government spheres and the media world. Now, these philosophers raise their voices and contrive to get to the root of the evil. There is, they say to us, a time of politics which requires that we look far ahead and act for the future. How can this be preserved from subjection to the temporal rhythm of the media, which lives solely from the present and from the obligation to sell something new every day? Public life must be held apart from the turpitudes of private life and private life shielded from the public eye. The institutions of common life rest on a symbolism that must not be interfered with. Politics is founded on distance. When we try to subject it to the media reign of visibility and total publicity, it is menaced by death. The concern for transparency is the great enemy of politics.

As our philosophers are impartial, they do not hesitate to call into question a member of their corporation. Jean-Jacques Rousseau was the one, they claim, who had this fatal idea of having transparency in common life. It was he who created the utopias and crimes of revolutionary virtue and fed the Terror conducted by the Incorruptible Robespierre. In the era of glasshouses and of small Soviet heroes denouncing the counter-revolutionary activities of their parents, this same idea of transparency came to engender totalitarian horror. Today, it takes the more anodyne form of the crowds of democratic society and their appetite for the secrets of princes and of the private lives of the stars. But the totalitarian worm is in the democratic fruit. It is to satisfy the appetites of the individuals of mass society that journalists deliver to them the fate of those in charge of our life in common and make the bed for the soft totalitarianisms of tomorrow. Before it is too late, then, let us restore the secrecy and distance that befits good Republican government.

This discourse, all the same, leaves us dreamy-eyed. What dictatorship was ever founded on transparency? The Stalinist regime may have erected statues of the young Pavel Morozov, killed by his family for having denounced his father. It was nonetheless founded on the systematic usage of secrecy, to the point of the existence of a Constitution which those whom it concerned had no way of finding out about. Some religious-type communities can be governed by the principle of transparency. No state is and totalitarian states less than all the others. Behind the fallacious equation Rousseauism = glasshouse = totalitarianism, this line of reasoning aims in fact to establish the idea according to which democracy is equal to the triumph of mass individualism, oblivious to the symbolic forms of public life but avid for publicity as for commodities. It is then easy to see in this democracy the principle of a contempt for politics that opens the path to totalitarianism. And it is easy to set in contrast to it some Republican virtue, which gazes high and far towards the great goals of common life, embodied in the service of the state.

At this point the governments take over again from the philosophers. After all, they remark, to what do we owe the corruption which reigns in the public marketplace? Are politicians using their municipal powers to extort money from companies in order to finance their party's expenses? But what, then, is the reason for these expenses if not the ruinous electoral campaigns during which we must stage publicity parades to satisfy the depraved taste of individuals of the democratic mass? Ought we do away with parties and elections? This is hypocritical, you see! The people of democratic individuals should have the honesty to accept this evil that it itself makes necessary. And even if some public monies inadvertently fall into the pockets of a few elected officials, it should recognize in these individual excesses the exaggerated image of its ordinary appetites. Because of it, elected republicans must sometimes divert their attention away from the great ends of common life on which they are normally affixed and engage in a bit of fishy business. Our virtue, in being compromised in this way, pays the price of the people's vice. The people should, in return, have the honesty to pay the price for the sacrifices we make. And it should not be allowed, with its hypocritical condemnations of a corruption whose cause it is, to exacerbate further the dangers with which it burdens the political cause and pave the way for totalitarianism!

So, everything transpires as if proof by corruption now functions the other way round. Formerly, this proof censured governments in the name of the people for betraying common affairs to serve their own private interests. Today, corruption serves to prove that governments are unpleasantly impeded in the running of common affairs due to the bad tendencies of the democratic people. The details of the argumentation count for less, then, than for what it must prove, namely that it is necessary to let those, whose affair it is, govern in peace. No doubt men of power only expose themselves so often to the desires of the petty democrats, greedy for the scandalous secrets of power, so as to bring this logic to completion. The media, in effect, only ever spreads the secrets that they are given. The people who asked the American president for the anatomical details concerning the exact nature of his relationship with Monika Lewinsky were not journalists in the service of the *people* press. They were good Christians, and honest judges and representatives, defenders of peace for families and of the secrecy of private life. And the cassette that contained the details about the secret financing of the French president's party was passed through the hands of a socialist minister before spreading to public space. Those who disclose the secrets are also those who exploit them for the purpose of muddling the affairs of the collective with their own or their party's. They therefore make alternate appeals to the advantages of the state secret and to those of the media transparency which denounces it. Since it is necessary to condemn, as the gravediggers of political virtue, the journalists to whom they convey their information and the readers who read it, and be able to appeal to their colleagues' solidarity in the face of 'media lynching' and misuses of democracy. So, added the advantages of the secret and those of its denunciation are those of the denunciation of denunciation. This closes the circle, then, whereby the very fact of corruption serves to prove that state affairs must not be subject to too much scrutiny since it risks endangering the Republic. In this twisted logic, those that it concerns manages to see themselves clear without too much trouble. As for the philosophers, that's another matter.

CHAPTER FIFTEEN
Voici/Voilà: The Destiny of Images,
January 2001

'The modern', Mallarmé once said, 'disdains to imagine'. Disdaining images obviously did not entail the adoration of solid realities. On the contrary, it meant making a contrast between the forms or performances of art and the confections of doubles of persons or of things. 'Nature has taken place; it can't be added to', he also once said. The poem or the painting must be the tracing of a specific act, the model for which Mallarmé found in the mute hieroglyphs contoured by the steps of the ballerina. So understood, the Mallarmean expression can quite usefully sum up an entire idea of artistic modernity. During the times of supre-matism, of futurism or of constructivism, this idea was keenly wed to the project of constructing new forms of life. With the disillusionment of these great hopes, it found its emblem in the purity of non-figurative painting, which counterposed the logic of coloured forms to all produc-tions of images that are bound to the consumption of resemblances.

Some time ago already, this identification of artistic modernity and its rejection of images came under challenge. But this is not to say that landscapes, naked women and still lives began to flourish once more on the walls of galleries and exhibitions. If the 'compositions' of the abstract age tended to recede, the upshot was not a newly figurative style of painting. Instead, it was a confrontation between images of the world with themselves. This principle was neatly encapsulated by three recent Parisian exhibitions. First up, the *Musée d'Art Moderne de la Ville de Paris* presented an exhibition titled *Voilà: Le Monde dans la tête*. The *Centre Georges-Pompidou* then followed suit with an exhibition called *Au-delà du spectacle.* Then at the *Centre national de la photographie* an exhibition opened called *Bruit de fond.* This quasi-simultaneousness is significant not due to any novelties that these exhibitions may have introduced but, on the contrary, due to their similarity to many other exhibitions throughout the world, to their common way of testifying today to what is commonplace in art.

The titles are already significant in themselves. 'Voilà' in French is the demonstrative that refers to the past or the distant. And, in actual fact, the exhibition strove to provide a sort of memoir of the century. Of the century as such and not of its art. In the installations of Christian Boltanski or of On Kawara, in the 1920s photographs by August Sander or the recent ones by Hans-Peter Feldmann, in the films of Jonas Mekas or of Chantal Ackerman, and in all the other installations, videos, photographic display cabinets or computers spread throughout the exhibition, the stake concerned our ways of taking and living with images. Neither did the room dedicated to painting deviate from this principle. In it, the exhibiting artist, Bertrand Lavier, did not in actual fact present *his* own paintings. He exhibited a series of all styles of paintings whose sole principle of unity was their signature: in fact, all the paintings gathered carried the same family name, the most widespread name in France, Martin. So, the art exhibition presented itself as identical to an archival work and visiting it to leafing through an encyclopaedia in which texts and images stand as testimonies of a time and as ways of apprehending this time and registering its signs. The contemporary art museum itself thus tends to oscillate between yesteryear's 'cabinet of curiosities' and an ethnological museum of our own civilizations.

The titles of two other exhibitions were explicitly borrowed from books. *Au-delà du spectacle* appealed to Guy Debord's essay *La Sociéte du spectacle,* and *Bruit de fond* to the homonymous novel by Don Delillo.[1] The banner under which both thus placed themselves is that of the critique of the world of media and publicity, illustrated by the theoretician of Situationism as by the novelist of the strange events orchestrated through television in the small town of Blacksmith. They testify to a type of art which no longer counterposes the purity of forms with the commerce of images. Forms can be opposed to images, so long as the latter appear as the superfluous double of things. But the concept of spectacle implies that images are no longer doubles of things, but the things themselves, the reality of a world in which things and images are no longer able to be distinguished. Wherever the image no longer stands opposite the thing, form and image become indistinguishable from one another. As such the contrast becomes one between the image and another sort of image. But another sort of image is not an image of different content. It is an image that is differently arranged, presented in another perceptual arrangement. Thus, in *Au-delà du spectacle* paintings were contrasted with media images. And if *Bruit de fond* presented photographs, it was not as works of photographers; it was as materials that artists integrate into arrangements whose function is to instruct us how to read images and to play with them.

Play and learn form an opposition that progressist pedagogues have never ceased to want to overcome. If *Voilà*'s installations evoked curiosity cabinets, those of *Au-delà du spectacle* could be likened to the design of a playful pedagogy. Indeed, along side a billiard table, a giant baby foot and a fairground merry-go-round, there were monitors, small cabins and doll houses crowding around, confronting visitors either with publicity icons reworked in a different medium, or with icons reproduced *tel quel* but outside their ordinary environment. The critical use of images thus tends to a certain minimalism. Photomontages of former times would play on the contradictory relation between two forms of iconography. In the 1930s, for example, John Heartfield x-rayed Hitler-the-orator to make visible the circulation of gold that fed the Nazi machine. And 40 years later Martha Rosler would stick scenes of the war in Vietnam onto images of American advertising narcissism. Today, the simple act of re-exhibiting identical images of advertising narcissism is itself attributed a critical value. It is as if all that is required to turn images of commodities and of power into critical instruments is to present them in a different space, teaching spectators to hold the noises and the collective images that condition their existence at a distance. In practice, the plaques introducing each work were made to manifest this difference, in reasserting in a quasi-incantatory manner the critical virtue of apparatuses of image displacement.

Art-archive, art-school: Against these two commonplace figures of an art comprised of images whose radicality is supposedly won by their similitude with images of the world, there periodically returns the nostalgia of an art which institutes a co-presence between humans and things and between humans themselves. At the *Palais des Beaux-Arts de Bruxelles* an exhibition of 'one hundred years of contemporary art', whose title manifests its polemical intention, opened recently under the auspices of the critic and theoretician Thierry de Duve. Against the *Voilà* of the Parisian exhibition, the Brussels exhibition counterposed a *Voici*. 'Voici' in French is the demonstrative of the presence of the present. The exhibition thus presents itself as the manifesto of a modern art conceived as an art of presence and of the gaze, as a *facingness* opposed to the formal *flatness* valorized by the grand theoretician of pictorial modernity, Clement Greenberg.[2] In it one sought in vain, however, for any old-style portraits, group scenes or still lives. Many of the works enlisted under the banner of the *Voici* could have easily featured under that of *Voilà*, including: portraits of stars by Andy Warhol, hyperrealist photographic compositions by Jeff Wall, documents of the mythical 'section of eagles' of the fictional museum by Marcel Broodthaers, the installation of a collection of GDR commodities by Joseph Beuys, peel off posters by Raymond Hains, mirrors by Pistoletto or a 'family album' by Christian Boltanski . . . More, the bodies of many of the works taken from minimalist sculpture or from *arte povera* were somewhat too frail to incarnate the splendours of the *facingness* evoked.

In sum, neither the gaze nor its object bear clear-cut criteria for differentiating between *voici* and *voilà*. What is required, then, is a supplement of discourse to transform the *ready-made* in the display unit or the smooth parallelepiped into mirrors of intersecting gazes. Minimalist sculptures or hyperrealist photographs thus have to be set under the authority of the supposed father of modern painting, Manet. But this father of modern painting must himself be set under the authority of the word made flesh. Manet's modernism – and that of all painting following it – is defined here on the basis of a painting from his youth rated as a primitive scene. During his 'Spanish' period, at the start of the 1860s, Manet painted his *Christ mort soutenu par les anges* in imitation of Ribalta. But contrary to the model, the eyes of Manet's Christ are open and he is facing the spectator. Nothing more is required, in our era of 'the death of God', to confer on painting a function of substitution. The dead Christ reopens his eyes, he resurrects in the pure immanence of pictorial presence and writes down in advance monochrome paintings as well as pop imagery, minimalist sculptures as well as fictional museums in the tradition of the icon and the religious economy of the resurrection.

'The image will come at the time of the Resurrection'. Saint Paul's expression provides the leitmotiv for Godard's *Histoire(s) du cinéma*. In it, he develops a theory of the image in which the white screen is transformed into Veronica's veil and Hitchcock's shots into icons of the pure presence of things. On either side of yesterday's formalism, it is two new forms of identification of art with the image that have been established: an art of the re-exhibition of ordinary images of the world and an art that contrasts them to the pure icons of presence. The paradox is that exactly the same works can be used to illustrate these antagonistic theorizations. This paradox is perhaps harshest for the theoreticians of presence. Their dream of immanence may only come about through self-contradiction: that of a discourse which transforms every piece of art into a little host, a morceau detached from the great body of the Word made flesh.

CHAPTER SIXTEEN
From Facts to Interpretations: The New Quarrel over the Holocaust, *April 2001*

An atmosphere of scandal hovers around the work of Peter Novick (*The Holocaust in American Life*) and of Norman Finkelstein (*The Holocaust Industry*). The latter indeed has triggered a violent polemic in the United States and England, and now in Germany and France. Here is a Jew, son of an Auschwitz survivor, who violently denounces the political, ideological and financial exploitation of the genocide by large Jewish organizations. His virulence has met with a violent reaction of rejection in which the author is accused of negationism. A slanderous accusation, he replies: a negationist is someone who denies the existence of the holocaust. Now, for his part, he resolutely affirms the existence of the holocaust, in lower case, as historical fact. What he denounces, on the other hand, is the Holocaust, in upper case, that is, the ideological elaboration of the holocaust as a unique event, of incomparable nature to any other historical form of massacre or genocide, specifically linked to the Gentiles' ancestral hatred against the Jews, and which, by the same token, justifies an unconditional support for the state of Israel and its policies – which also means for the Federal American state, whose own support for Israel would absolve it of all wrongdoing against the Indians and the Blacks of America, as well as against the Vietnamese children burnt by napalm or the starved Iraqi children.

If the contradictors were hardly satisfied by this response, this is because the negationist affair brought to light the problematic nature of the simple distinction between facts and interpretations of facts. An historical fact is constituted as such by the interpretation that links a multiplicity of material facts together. One of the pioneers of negationism, the Frenchman Paul Rassinier, himself a survivor of the Buchenwald camp, gave the first demonstration of it in the 1950s. He denied neither that regular selections were made in the camps nor the presence of gas chambers. He simply cast doubt on the connection between the two. He was even ready to accept the idea that there effectively were gassings. He simply cast doubt on the question of whether they were part of a overall design.

The documents gathered since then have shown the injustice of these quibbles. But if negationism still remains, and if today someone who recognizes the reality of the Nazi extermination of Europe's Jews can be accused of negationism, then it is because the tracing of the border separating 'facts' and 'interpretations' is more twisted than it first appears. Where do we place the border that enables us to affirm the constituted fact as such, in its self-sufficiency, and to discard every other additional connection as an extrinsic interpretation? If the polemic over the exceptionality of the massacre of Europe's Jews seems interminable, it is owing to a conflict between two contradictory requirements. If the holocaust is to be considered an indisputable fact, it must be isolated in its raw factuality, outside of every interpretative debate on the reasons for which it was placed on the Nazi agenda. But if its reality is to be considered that of the anti-Jewish holocaust, the interpretation must, conversely, trace it back to a first cause, to a necessary and sufficient reason, and establish that what was at work in the death camps was an original will to exterminate the Jews. But where is this first cause to be located? The mere delirium of a head of state or of a group of fanatics does not constitute a necessary reason. This reason is identified by theoreticians concerned with proving the holocaust as radical singularity with the Gentiles' age-old hatred of Jews. The reality of the holocaust is therefore held to be indissociable from a determinate interpretation. But at this point the argument turns around: why did this ancient and universal hatred take the specific form that it did in this country and at this historical moment, a form which, moreover, we know was also applied to other categories of 'degenerates': the mentally ill, homosexuals, gypsies?

Thus, the dialectic of the fact and the 'intention' redoubles to infinity and acts to cast suspicion on the exact intentions of anyone who stops the chain of connections at any given point. Thus, regarding the thesis of immemorial hatred, Finkelstein denounces the subordination of facts to an interested interpretation. For him, linking the holocaust to an ineradicable, exterminatory will is tantamount to justifying, in all aspects, the Israeli state's politics of self-preservation and the US policy of support. But it is not the bare nudity of facts that he brings to bear against the scenario that he denounces; it is another scheme of interpretation, namely the classic scenario of suspicion which inquires into the hidden reason as to why one speaks so much about this fact or that sufferance, and invariably concludes that it is to hide others. In Finkelstein's discourse, the 'Holocaust' thus becomes the cover which enables Israel to continue despoiling the Palestinians and America to forget the massacres and injustices that have stamped its history. But the suspicion over the 'intention' immediately turns back on him: relating the holocaust dead not to the cause of the massacre but to the exterminated American Indians or the bombarded Vietnamese means dissolving the facts in the long history of human atrocities in which everything levels out and is made equivalent in order to weaken Israel's moral position against the Palestinians.

However, the problem cannot be reduced to an exchange of unverifiable arguments between the partisans of Israel and of Palestine. The internalization of the quarrel over negationism refers to two deeper intellectual phenomena. First of all, it concerns the splitting of our idea of reality. Proving the real today is carried out twice over: phenomena are inserted in a chain of causes and effects, and, conversely, are shown to be brute in character, lacking in reason. If this duality constitutes the core of the theoretical conflict over the holocaust, this is no doubt because the process of the extermination and of the programmed disappearance of its traces has obliged the long detour of argumentative reconstruction to confirm the reality of the facts. But it is also because the impossibility of assigning a necessary and sufficient reason works to undermine the rationality of political and scientific phenomena.

It is symptomatic that the present attacks against the 'holocaust industry' come from an American Jewish Marxist. This latter presents himself as a sort of last of the Mohicans, remaining loyal to the tradition of progressivism to which the Jewish émigrés to the United States subscribed. But he does so not only by laying claim to a political tradition. It is more a tradition of interpretation that he defends: one that links political and ideological phenomena to social causes, and local facts – regardless of their singularity or enormity – to the global entanglement of causes and interests. The quarrel over the holocaust challenges the validity of glo- balist explanations of a socio-economic type, against which some irre- ducible irrational element is brought to bear, whether raw facts or a primordial hatred that serves as their cause. Behind an American Marx- ist Jew's rage against his peers there lies the singular ideological config- uration of the present, that in which new radical forms of world domination are escorted by a publicly announced prohibition on the forms of global explanation that pretend to have their measure.

It is thus possible to understand the singular temporality according to which the Nazi genocide was transformed *après coup* into an historical cut. Novick and Finkelstein recall that after 1945 the holocaust was not greatly present in western consciousness. They attribute the reversal in spirit to the Israeli-Arab war and to the Israeli victory of 1967. However, more than this, it was in the 1990s that the vision of the holocaust as an event that cut the history of the world into two imposed itself. This ret- rospective cut clearly marks the mourning of another cut in the history of the world, the one that was called revolution, and whose last avatars crumbled with the fall of the Soviet empire and the disappointed expecta- tion of not seeing a regenerated democracy emerge from its ruins. It is in this context that the holocaust's irreducibility has become emblematic of the rejection of the Marxist conception of history, conceived as the global rationality of historical facts and as a temporality oriented by a promise of emancipation. Invocations of the Gentiles' 'immemorial' hatred of the Jews and assertions of the impossibility, after Auschwitz, of thinking and living as before, amount to much more than the interested arguments condemned by Finkelstein. They carry out an emblematic overturning of the direction of time, opposing the promises of a hypothetical future to an immemorial past which never passes. If the explanation is so violent that pits the partisans of the exceptionality of the Jewish genocide against those who want to integrate it into the great historical and worldwide interweaving of cases, it is because it brings together the two avatars of militant certainties and of yesterday's historical expectation. One side has inverted the great promise into the weight of an immemorial past, the other wants to uphold its vigour, were it by simple argumentative fury. The quarrel over the holocaust is also a mourning of revolutionary thought. This is why a simple knowledge of the facts cannot come close to resolving the quarrel over intentions.

CHAPTER SEVENTEEN
From One Torture to Another, *June 2001*

What provokes our indignation today and what face do we give to the intolerable? Some weeks ago, France was shaken by the return of a not very old repressed. Général Aussares, commander of the French special services during the Algerian war, revealed the details of the systematic practice of torturing suspects that was carried out by the intelligence services. Reveal is going a bit too far. More than 40 years ago, writers and teachers took up their plumes to denounce the methods that the special service was employing. Their books were banned or prosecuted, and the governments, socialist and then Gaullist, which conducted the war in Algeria, treated these revelations as fabrications designed to demoralize the troops and the nation in order to aid the Algerian insurrection. So one may find comic the horrified declarations by Jacques Chirac and the socialist ministers expressing outrage at this abominable torturer – himself a simple executor of the policy devised by the heads of state or government of which they are the inheritors. Those who condemned the torture in Algeria forgot to mention that the affair was not about the scheming of a perverted military official but a policy of a state, a policy of the reason of state that justifies everything and of the state secrecy that provides cover for it.

So, this 'revelation' of a broadly known secret put today's government leaders, who are the sons of yesterday's leaders, in an uncomfortable position. Fortunately, the capacities of public indignation would soon fixate on a wholly different object of contemporary scandal. A private French television station launched a programme called *Loft Story*, modelled on the Dutch *Big Brother,* which had already been adapted in several other countries. Eleven young people were confined under the eye of cameras which then continuously broadcast the episodes of their encaged lives: anodyne conversations, grooming rituals and erotic frolics. The ensemble of this (in)activity was simultaneously centered around the aim of the game: the progressive elimination of the loft's occupants – by internal pre-selection and the vote of viewers – until only a single couple – the winning couple – was left. Within a few days, all audience records were broken. Also within a few days, journalistic and intellectual opinion had scrutinized this new 'phenomenon of society'. The dominant tone was one of indignation. This indignation was sometimes limited to the economic and cultural aspects of the affair: here were people paid a minimum wage to provide an image of life as it is – this is simultaneously a new form of work exploitation and a way of reducing the expenses of the cultural industry to a strict minimum, necessary to bring in advertising revenues. 'Money has brushed aside culture' declared a left weekly newspaper. Most often, however, the condemnation bore on much more than some infringement of the industrial relations legislation; it decried the accomplishment of the totalitarian system. These guinea pigs, shut up day and night under the eye of the camera, displaying their private lives to the gaze of all, this sham community with no other goal than to eliminate the others, was this not the accomplishment of the great dream of total control over the lives of individuals? In the columns of *Le Monde*, one philosopher drew the consequence from it: *Loft Story* portrayed the 'terrible but tame ideal of the society that totalitarianism had dreamt of without being able to fulfil it'.[1] In vain did one draw to the attention of the prophets of final catastrophe that there were some slight differences between the 11 competitors of *Loft Story* and the millions of prisoners of the Stalinist or Nazi camps. These latter had not chosen to be held where they were, and those who had locked them up were not preoccupied with making spectacles of their lives but, on the contrary, with relegating it to the shadows. Lastly, instead of mass extermination, slow extermination or psychic destruction, the lucky winners were promised a villa. Such details would not trouble the condemners: they responded that this is exactly what perfected totalitarianism is, a 'soft totalitarianism' that does not perform any torture and does not destroy any bodies, but which is exercised 'only on minds, only in images'.

We recognize the logic of the argument: the more invisible the effect, the more proven is the cause. Ironically, this paranoid logic has always been that of totalitarian powers. The procurer Vichinsky would use it to identify the most perverted saboteurs of the Soviet homeland: those who concealed the fact that they were saboteurs by not getting involved in any acts of sabotage. Similarly, the more immaterial it is, or the more internal its effects, the more perfect totalitarianism is reputed to be. By the same token, the stories of torture, or state reason and secrecy can be made to disappear without a trace. Totalitarianism, we are taught today, is the internalized law of generalized transparency. In the age of planetary publicity, we are all confined, all in camps, victims of the pure, accomplished logic of the system that old-style torturers and heads of extermination camps could only approach in amateurish fashion.

Not long ago, Michel Foucault feared the simplistic consequences that might be drawn from his theses on 'control society'. He feared that all the world's political persecutions would find themselves dissolved in a night of 'confinement' in which all cows were grey. He bemoaned an utterly convenient way of saying: 'We all have our Gulag: it is there at our doors, in our towns, in our hospitals, in our prisons. It is here in our heads'.[2] This fear was certainly justified. Since then, discourses did not cease to develop, some even making reference to Foucault's 'biopolitics' as a cover, that subsume the most diverse atrocities of state reason under the concept of 'soft' totalitarianism – which is everywhere, but first of all and especially on television screens and in the heads of television viewers. To denounce the commerce of images has become the foremost of duties – and the least costly of 'heroisms'.

To be sure, the promoters of these programmes did not launch their products to have us forget genocides and tortures. And neither do the denunciatory philosophers mean them to be forgotten. But in the raging polemic, a strange consensus is established between the image merchants, the condemners of the image and the government. The latter, always bothered by the return of repressed episodes of state reason, indulgently welcomed these 'totalitarian' programmes. The television viewer of ordinary everyday life, offered up the consumption of ordinary individuals, is a perfect match for their current motto: everyday realism in the service of the daily preoccupations of 'citizens'. 'Getting in touch' and 'community politics', the present-day key words of our governments, herein find their most precise illustration. The old representation of the state and the political condemnation of its 'reason' and secrecy is substituted for a twofold description of our society. On the one hand, society is presented as the seat of peaceful and run-of-the-mill preoccupations, of little problems and small pleasures, whose pacifying virtues are counterposed to the social and democratic tumult accused of creating the great totalitarian catastrophes. Society is thus most harmoniously suited to the modest state management of today, liquidator of grand utopias. But, on the other, this society of the 'everyday', of 'listening' and of 'proximity' is presented as the supreme form of a totalitarianism whose seat is none other than the narcissism of the ordinary democratic individual, epitomized by the television viewer. So, on the one hand, there is the wise and realist management state set in opposition to the 'totalitarianism' born of the utopian passions of popular ferment. While, on the other, the noble Republican state, guarantor of the symbolic order and of universalist values, is summonsed to contain the 'totalitarianism' inherent in the narcissism of democratic individuals. On both hands, then, the reason of state is discretely lightened of the load of its real crimes and is legitimated anew against those of an imaginary totalitarianism.

CHAPTER EIGHTEEN

The Filmmaker, the People and the Government,
August 2001

Among the feature films of the Venice Film Festival is *L'Anglaise et le Duc,* a period piece by Eric Rohmer, inspired by the memoirs of an aristocratic Englishwoman living under the French Revolution.[1] Rumours have it that the Italian festival is thus paying tribute to a film that the French selectors of the Festival of Cannes allegedly rejected for reasons of political correctness. A scent of scandal and of repression never does any harm to a film but this time it calls for reflection. For what reason would it be compromising today to film Revolution in general and the French Revolution in particular from the viewpoint of aristocrats? For decades, French children have devoured – without any damage having been done to Republican and revolutionary values – the stories of the *Mouron rouge,* a heroic English aristocrat who saves gentle nobles from the clutches of the ferocious popular brutes. And since the 1980s the theses of Francois Furet, largely inspired by the counter-revolutionary tradition, have dominated revolutionary historiography and intellectual opinion in France. One does not therefore see what considerations of political correctness would prevent the showing of bloodthirsty revolutionaries today. And one suspects that those who make Rohmer to be the artistic flag-bearer of a France that is finally confronting its revolutionary phantoms by simply using the classic trick of presenting the dominant vision of things as a minority viewpoint, a victim of persecution in a horrible 'plot by intellectuals'.

But if there is a politics in this film, perhaps it plays out elsewhere than in these flag fights. Rohmer has never tried to pass himself off as a man of the left. And he maintains that he did not want to make a militant film. Indeed, the story of Grace Elliot's adventures in the revolutionary torment is little concerned to judge the causes and effects of the Revolution. By way of doctrine, it presents only two commonplaces of political and historical fiction. The first contrasts moral and affective fidelity to the tortuous calculations of politics. In this way, the English Lady embodies the feminine and unthinking virtue of fidelity to the persecuted Royal family, in the face of the masculine vice of calculating self-interest, represented by the Duke of Orleans, one of the King's cousins and a man who is prepared to make any compromise to serve his own dynastic interests, including voting for the death of his cousin. The second commonplace opposes the good manners of evolved people to the eternal uncouthness of the bestial populace. Some used to counterpose the correctness of German officers to the sadism of the SS brutes. Similarly, Grace Elliot is continuously wrenched from the hands of the concupiscent and inebriated hordes by officers or commissaries, indeed by representatives of the people of Robespierre, to remind the populace of the sense of the laws and of the civility of worldly decency. So, if there is a political message in the film, it does not concern the legitimacy or the illegitimacy of revolutions. It boils down to the rather widespread, two-fold idea that politics is a dirty thing and that this dirty thing must remain the preserve of those who have proper clothing and civil manners, that it must be placed out of reach of the street population.

Of course, Rohmer is no ideologue. He is a filmmaker. But this is exactly where things become interesting. In his film, the relation between the proper and the dirty, between respectable people and the street crowd, is turned into a problem of occupying the image. This problem is raised and solved in aesthetic and technical terms which have an emblematic value. The film in fact has a pictorial backdrop, drawn from aquarelles representing the Paris at the end of the eighteenth century, with its aristocratic 'sweetness of living', which had just been drastically altered by the Revolution. All the exterior scenes and in particular the crowd scenes were filmed in the studio against a neutral background and were then inset into this painted canvass setting. This procedure is not merely an economic alternative to the costly reconstitution of decors from the epoch. It is also a manner of staging the people and of putting it back in its place. This setting, which is made for the passage of carriages, is best suited for the two or three picturesque characters that conventionally establish the scale of the monuments and inject some life into it. Only, at this point, the canvass in some sense opens up and instead of these genteel bit players there emerges a compact crowd, which, visibly, has no place being there. The visual arrangement of the *mise-en-scène* thus presents the allegory of the 'bad' politics: that where the streets normally designed for traffic between public edifices and private residences become the theatre in which the crowd of anonymous bit players improperly proclaims itself the political people.

But this arrangement corrects the excess that it manifests. These crowds of common men of sinister appearance, who invade the palaces of kings and the hotels of nobles, are assembled in the studio by the filmmaker between ropes fixed to prevent their digitalized images from entering inopportunely into the painted décor. Thus, the painted image, the studio and the digital camera combine their powers to resolve aesthetically a political problem, or rather the very problem of politics itself: the fact that these street people, though *visibly* not destined to do so, concern themselves with common affairs.

Things are evidently less easy for those we call *politicians.* And perhaps the Venice film jury, in beholding Rohmer's framed and digitalized crowds, bore a compassionate thought for the statesmen of the G8 who had gathered at Genoa only 2 months beforehand. For the latter, who would like to govern the world in only having to deal with responsible 'interlocutors' – be they dictators or former KGBers like Putin – still have no ways of performing any studio channelling or digital dissolving on the crowds of demonstrators who persist in thinking that they are also part of the world and have a vocation to concern themselves with its affairs. Nor does showing demonstrators in hoods – the modern equivalent of the bestial face of rioters of yesteryear – suffice to put the people in its place. So it is necessary to entrust the police with the 'aesthetic' task of cleaning up the streets, in transforming historical towns into bunkers, in charging down demonstrators and in invading their Headquarters, and in a much less civil manner than the Parisian Sectionaries in Rohmer's film invade the dwelling of the beautiful Englishwoman. According to the well-known joke, being unable to build cities in the country, the greats of this world have therefore decided to gather next time in the Canadian mountains, so that, far from the noises of the unwelcome crowd, they can realize their own dream, the current dream of governments: the direction between responsible men of a world without people.

So, if Rohmer's film provokes embarrassment, it is not because it clashes with the spirit of the times. On the contrary, it is because it is too conformist to this world, because, beneath its visually and ideologically *retro* appearance, it images in too direct a manner the contemporary dream of the world government of 'competent' people, delivered of all disturbances from the street. Once again, Rohmer is little concerned to play the flag-bearer for the final burial of revolutions. His politics is first and foremost aesthetic. His own 'counter-revolution' is circumscribed within the field of cinema. Though he never played at being a leftist, in the 1950s he was one of the first champions of the Rossellinian revolution whose principles ended up paving the way for the 'New Waves': bid farewell to the studios and go into the streets with the cameras on the search contemporary inhabitants of the world, chasing all the unforeseen events that make up their material, sentimental and possibly political itineraries. Following the mobile camera of New Wave filmmakers, students of the 1960s set out to discover the social world of their time and invaded the streets of Paris and a few other metropolises. Again, this link between an aesthetics of the cinema and a way of practicing politics is also evoked by Godard's last film, *Éloge de l'amour,* in which the camera travels through the streets of Paris, visits the night cleaners of trains as though it were a leftist handing out pamphlets, and places itself meditatively before the building, today deserted, of the erstwhile 'worker fortress' at the Renault factories. As for Rohmer, he turned away from the hazards of the streets very early on to dedicate himself to the ups and downs of sentiment in socially protected microcosms, but all the same without renouncing Rossellinian realism. The avowed artificialism which corresponds, in *L'Anglaise et le Duc,* to an historic broadening of the set, today works as an aesthetic manifesto symbolically closing an age of cinema. It is in this, more than in any ideological measure, that he is in agreement with the desire to close, finally, an age which wanted to return to the streets and render politics to all.

CHAPTER NINETEEN
Time, Words, War, *November 2001*

'Between good and evil, we know that God is not neutral'. These were the words with which George Bush announced his confidence in the US-launched anti-terrorist war. The argument obviously raises some problems, the first of which might be simply expressed: God actually does seem strangely neutral in the affair. The same God, that of Moses/Moussa and of Abraham/Ibrahim, supports the opposite conviction: that the Jihad combatants will triumph in their good cause against the evil American empire. The causes are expressed by each side in moral and religious language. And this language is also often used by the opponents to the crusade announced by the president of the United States. The terms *'God', 'Love', 'Peace', 'No more hate',* were to be read practically everywhere on the inscription-covered posters carried by those gathered, in Union Square or in Washington Square, to bring the solicitude of the God of love to bear against the fury of the God of vengeance: 'Let us not become the evil that we deplore'. As if it were admitted that only in such religious and moral terms can a distance be taken with respect to the great consensus of the nation united around its victims and their vengeance. But it is not simply a question of respect and of solidarity towards the victims. More radically, everything transpires as if the words that were traded 30 years ago – free world, imperialism, oppression, resistance . . . – have no more currency, as if no other language, no other framework of thought were available to articulate and judge the situation.

That this is so at the beginning of the third millennium, in the core of the 'advanced world', calls for reflection. A while ago already, the

soothsayers proclaimed the end of politics and history. This end, however, bears meagre resemblance to the one that they proclaimed. The
'end of history' proclaimed by Francis Fukuyama, and soon confirmed
by the fall of the Soviet Empire, bespoke the end of a world that had
been divided into opposing blocs by the socialist alternative. The end
of utopias – another grand theme of the 1980s – bespoke the end itself of
the gap between the ideals of justice and the empirical administration of
necessities. Democracy had imposed itself as the ultimate form of government, the rational government able to make the demands of justice
coincide with economic necessity. Where utopia had created division,
the return to a shared set of givens about a restrictive reality appeared to
promise, in the more or less distant long term, agreement within nations
and among nations. Sure enough some expressed their discordance,
their voices breaking through the consensual music of official political
scientists. These voices set against this all-too-simple realism, the advent
of a virtual, media world, where every reality vanishes into images and
every image into numbers. The ones welcomed the reign of communication for its ability to destroy economic and state fortresses and establish,
within this situation of generalized intermixing, the great planetary
democracy of networking. The others denounced the limitless extension
of the society of control, the collapse of the real, the soft totalitarianism
of the total screen, or the fatal triumph of the narcissistic individual in
mass democracy. But these apparent dissidences rested on one and the
same essential belief. The naïve and the clever, the optimists and the
pessimists, at bottom shared the same idea – the charge so often levelled
at the now defunct communism: that of a unique sense of history in
which technology, economics and politics progress hand-in-hand, in
which the worldwide circulation of humans and commodities dooms
particularisms to vanish, in which the development of new technologies
spells the ruin of old ideologies.

The ethnic conflicts in the European East, the rise of fundamentalism
in the Muslim world and the rise of an extreme racist and xenophobic
right in several western countries were apparently not enough to shake
the belief in this temporal concordance. Would the collapse of the Twin
Towers be enough to shake it today? For a start, September 11 reminded
those who thought we now lived in the pure virtual universe of the network, and even those who said that the horror endured that day had
been anticipated one hundred times over by catastrophe films, that we

continue to live and work in buildings made of iron, glass or stone whose resistance or weaknesses have nothing to do either with screens or with special effects and that when they collapse they really do. Above all, it showed above all that the supreme weapon of carrying out real destruction was the very 'ideology' that the reality of the present-day world and the empire of technological communication were supposed to have relegated to the realm of memory. Behind the falsely naïve question 'Why do they hate us?', lies a dismay that is more sincere: 'Why are they not reasonable like us? Why don't things obey that simple reason according to which, when goods multiply, people live better and, if they live better, they become more peaceful?' We would like to believe that such attacks are perpetrated by those as yet unable to enjoy goods and well-being. But how are we to understand that someone can both be the head of an international financial network and a warrior of God, a suicidal fanatic and a meticulous organizer and executer? How can someone who is not miserable and does not have nothing left to lose, a man who is rather normal, has an education and is able to pursue a great career as an engineer, rush headlong toward a certain death?

So the present-day ruining of politics to the advantage of morality and religion cannot be put down to the 'end of history' scenario that has dragged on more or less everywhere for the last 20 years. It cannot be identified with the planetary reign of reasonable management setting itself up on the ruins of utopia. On the contrary, it marks not only the refutation of this 'reasonable' scenario, but also of the linear conception of historical evolution which underpins it. Politics is not over. It is simply absent. It is excluded in principle by authoritarian state forms, which claim bluntly not to need it because the word of God or some other principle of identity constitutes the true foundation of the life of communities. It is hollowed out from the inside by liberal states, which tend increasingly to reduce democratic forms to the reputedly univocal management of common economic interests. More than ever today, it appears that politics is not a permanent given assimilable to the organization of state communities. It is instead a singular way of conducting conflicts and of making them the very centre of life in common. This way is not always active. But, in addition, every state, whether good or bad, tends to effect a reduction of politics, whether by violent or mild means, in the name of an unambiguous, non-conflictual principle of community: that is, in the name of an identity of faith or origin, or of the law, the common interest or the force of circumstance.

Further, as politics tends to vanish, then it starts above all to appear as a way of providing events with a name and a framework, of understanding the difference of temporalities in one and the same present, of situating the same and the other in a common space. Some have no need of it, finding in the Holy Scriptures or the law of blood or soil something that caters for all necessities. Others, educated by political perceptions more than they might think, find they have been disarmed of it. This is what can be observed in the present-day United States and among its allies. Their recourse to the sure bearings of morality and religion translates the impossibility of giving a name to the conflict, of situating the enemy in a common space, of conceiving the common time of ancestral convictions that animates it and of new technologies that it wields to translate them into acts. The inability is shared by American leaders who do not know how to name their war and by opponents to the war, who do not know how to argue their opposition. Some might say that this is merely a question of words, which in no way hinders the game of power. But this simple opposition between words and acts also comes into question. The difficulties that American power has to contend with do not result simply from the inadaptability of its military means to Afghan geography but from the very nature of that power. American hegemony consists first of all in the hegemony it exercises over its allies in the name of the consensual logic of common interests and limitative realities. The same logic by which allied states are subordinated is the one by which they consolidate their own power. For those who accept the rules of the game, this logic is irrefutable. For those who reject it wholesale, it spins around in the void. In the heart of the superpower arises an impotence vastly different from the traditionally invoked difficulty of attuning domestic democratic life to the fight to death against an enemy that bars no holes. The same reasons which disarm protest in western states and give free reign to their government could well make it difficult for them not only to name their enemy and their war but also to bring it to an end.

CHAPTER TWENTY
Philosophy in the Bathroom, *January 2002*

La Philosophie comme manière de vivre, Petite Philosophie du matin, 101 Expéri-ences de philosophie quotidienne, Antimanuel de philosophie, The Consolations of Philosophy[1] . . . The philosopher perusing the titles featuring on the shelves of Parisian bookstores in this festive period would be agreeably satisfied by the fact that his idol compares favourably with Bin Laden as the star of editorial fashion. Philosophy is certainly most fashionable. A few years ago, this fashion was made by the success of philosophy-cafés where, with the help of a moderator, anyone at all could turn up on Sunday to debate the great questions of human existence. Then came the consultations of philosophy, philosophy in the service of company problems, and the successful day- or week-long philosophy seminars organized by various large and small towns, called to come and live the hour of philosophy.

At a second glance, of course, the philosopher asks himself a question: what exactly is this triumphant philosophy? And, being in the trade, he cannot fail to notice the dominant tone of this philosophical bookstore display. From philo-cafés to philosophy best-sellers, one and the same assertion is repeated over and over again. This assertion contrasts living philosophy, the one with which each of us can confront the problems of our concrete existence, to university philosophy, that which one teaches as a professor or studies to become a professor in turn. Some of the authors alluded to above are themselves part of the university corpora-tion. And yet they speak with the same voice as the others, in laying claim a style of philosophy that has descended from the university chair and into the world of life.

It remains only to find out what exactly this 'life' is to which philosophy has returned. The despondent never fail to note that this restoration of philosophy to all and sundry is also a way of confining all and sundry within their existential problems. 'University' philosophers such as Kant or Fichte confronted the all-powerful Theology Faculty, under the gaze of students dreaming of the French Revolution and of monarchs who might cancel their courses at any moment. The philosopher slumbering inside each of us, as for him, is asked to devote himself to other problems than those of founding the legitimacy of the state: that is, the 'true' problems that each of us encounters in daily life once we've left the concerns of justice and freedom to the specialists. The reader of Alain de Botton's *The Consolations of Philosophy* will first discover, with the example of Socrates, how not to suffer from one's 'lack of popularity'. After which the reader will have the liberty to find in Epicurus the means to resist money worries, in Montaigne those to endure sexual problems and in Schopenhauer the weapon with which to brave love disappointments. Philosophy is thereby returned to its function: to change the life of those who dedicate themselves to it. Forget the contradiction involved in contrasting living philosophy with its university history only ultimately to propose a few summaries or chosen texts from great philosophers. Because the privileged philosophers themselves – Socrates, Epicurus, Seneca, Montaigne, Schopenhauer – actually provide a demonstration of a philosophy for non-professionals, identical to the experiment of changing one's life.

The problem is only to know what life it is that is to be changed and what the extent of the change is. Nietzsche, who often applied Plato and was a passionate reader of Schopenhauer, had his own view of this. For him, the school of Socrates taught not the pleasures of a life preserved from popularity, but a new sort of combat sport by which to shine in the eyes of the world. It was of course a sport addressed to privileged amateurs: those young rich people who had nothing to do with their existence other than to turn it into a work of art. And the work of art *par excellence* by which they were fascinated, the new goal that philosophy assigned to their life, was the dying Socrates. To transform one's life and to make it philosophical by making philosophy become life meant learning to flee as quickly as possible, as far as possible.

To ask philosophy to be an art of living that remedies the little worries of existence, does this not, if taken seriously, always force it towards this goal: to take the seriousness away from these worries, and to take away one's belief in the imperatives of life to which they are linked? We can read Schopenhauer to learn how to relativize our heartaches. But Schopenhauer himself asks something else, which is that we escape from the vision of the world in which these heartaches makes themselves felt, that we learn not to want and to become spectators. Things can doubtless be stated more or less dramatically. There is nothing at all unpleasant, for example, in the *101 Experiments in the Philosophy of Everyday Life* proposed by Roger-Pol Droit: 'Wait without doing anything', 'Follow the movements of ants', 'Shower with your eyes closed', 'Exit the cinema in broad daylight', 'Wake up without knowing where', and 'Take the metro without going anywhere'. But we can surely see where all these exercises of sense disorientation lead. The philosophical experience of the strangeness of the world comes to term in the conviction that 'true life' is 'nothing but a fiction among others' which 'will come to an end in any case'.

Is this way of changing life really what is required at a time when each of us is encouraged to cast off all pessimism and make our enthusiastic contribution to the new life of the cyber-market, the euro and the grandiose mergers of the giants of planetary communication? Socrates and Schopenhauer are asked to lower their demands, to transform their ways of learning to leave this world into a way of 'living the everyday'. For this, all that is required is a little change in the meaning of the exercise. The journalist-philosopher encourages us to 'shower with your eyes closed', so that, unaware of where the gushing water is coming from, we are left only with the pure sensation of wet skin. The philosopher-journalist, author of the *Petite Philosophie du matin,* removes the suspect Schopenhauerian sophistication from these ablutions: 'Among the tonic acts of the morning, finishing your wash with a jet of cold water over the whole body is among the most stimulating', Christine Rambert assures us in the 127th of her '365 thoughts to be happy every day'.

This philosophy is certainly less perilous. It agrees perfectly with the multitude of recommendations that we are fed by doctors, psychologists, hygienists, nutritionists and others in hundreds of magazines and special programmes, teaching us how to take good care of our self and how to live life harmoniously in the everyday. The question that thus re-emerges is the following: is there really any need of philosophy if all it does is repeat the media refrain of the everyday care of the self? This is the heart of the problem: the advocates of 'philosophy in life' want simultaneously to enjoy the thrill of travelling in the Platonic chariot across the radiant heaven of Ideas and to have the half-hearted comfort of thought and body in the smallest things of life. Socrates renouncing the life of opinion and a water mixer.

In philosophical imagery, there is always one who gazes at the sky and one who gazes at the earth. To have the sky and the earth at once, we are no doubt obliged to turn towards other fictions. Alongside the philosophical consolations on offer on bookstore tables, another consoler began a new stage of her fabulous career through DVD. This consoler, the little Amélie Poulain, spearhead of the French cinematographic industry, solves the problematic marriage of the sky to which one flees and the earth in which one takes root. *Le Fabuleux Destin d'Amélie Poulain* presents an exemplary reconciliation of two opposite theses: first, you have to escape the greyness of reality into the ideal; second, you have to return from the ideal sky back into reality. On the one hand, Amélie is the little fairy who changes the lives of those around with her simple decision, assuaging their inconsolable hearts, unifying solitary souls, punishing the wicked, rewarding the good and moving the sedentary. But it would be all mere illusion if the one who projected her ideal sky into the lives of others did not also take care of herself and know how to cash in on her dreams for an occasion that has offered itself in prosaic reality and is certain never to be represented again, in the figure of young man who it seems is not very bright.

Fiction is more beautiful than reality. Reality is more beautiful than any fiction. Amélie has spectators participate in the enjoyment of that irrefutable philosophy by placing the Schopenhauerian experience of disorientation from the familiar world on the side of the villainous, racist greengrocer – whose slippers she swaps or whose toothpaste she replaces with foot-cream. She contrasts the equivocal experiences of philosophy to the happy union of the sky and the earth. No doubt quarrelsome minds will say that the union of the sky and the earth bears strong resemblance to the wedding of advertising and commodities and that this cheerful philosophy of the everyday recalls all too much the theology of the sensible/suprasensible commodity that, in another time, was analyzed by Marx.

CHAPTER TWENTY-ONE
Prisoners of the Infinite, *March 2002*

'Infinite Justice': this was the initial name given to the Pentagon's offensive against that fuzzy-contoured enemy denoted by the name 'terrorism'. As we know, the name was quickly corrected. It had been, we were led to understand, an excess of language on the part of a president still inexperienced in the art of nuance. If he wanted bin Laden 'dead or alive', it was obviously because he had watched too many Westerns in his youth.

This explanation is hardly convincing. For the 'dead or alive' principle is by no means that of Westerns. It is in actual fact commonplace in Westerns to see sheriffs risking their skin to wrench assassins from the lynch mob and hand them over to the system of justice. In contrast to the lessons of any Western, infinite justice is a justice without limits: a justice that ignores all the categories by which the exercise of justice is traditionally circumscribed: those which distinguish legal punishment from the vengeance of individuals, which separate the law from the political, the ethical or the religious; and which separate the police forms of tracking down crimes from the military forms of battles between armies. From this viewpoint, there was no excess of language. 'Nuances' would indeed be quite inappropriate. For it is exactly these features that characterize the retaliatory operations undertaken by the United States. These operations involve eliminating the differences that separate war and the police from all the legal forms by means of which we've sought to specify and limit the action of each of them. One no longer says 'dead or alive' except to say that nobody knows whether the individual concerned is, precisely, dead or alive. Yet no one knows exactly on what grounds the American military is detaining and aiming to try prisoners who benefit neither from prisoner of war status nor from the ordinary guarantees granted to defendants in the framework of a criminal case. The term 'infinite justice' says precisely what is at stake: the assertion of a right identical with the omnipotence hitherto reserved for the avenging God. The traditional distinctions, in fact, all wind up being abolished at the same time as the forms of international law are effaced.

Of course, this effacing is already the principle of terrorist action, which is equally indifferent to political forms and to the norms of law. But 'infinite justice' is not only the response to the adversary's provocation, a constraint to situate oneself on the same terrain as him. It also expresses that strange status that the effacing of the political today confers on law, both within and between nations.

Considerations of the current state of law reveal a singular inversion of things. In the 1990s, the Soviet empire's collapse and the weakening of social movements in major Western countries were generally celebrated as the liquidation of the utopias of real democracy and social democracy in favour of the rules of the State of Right. Outbursts of ethnic conflict and religious fundamentalism just as soon gainsaid this simple philosophy of history. But the identification of Western triumph with the triumph of the State of Right has likewise proven problematic. Within the Western powers and in their modes of foreign intervention, the relation between right and fact has actually evolved in such a way as to tend increasingly towards blurring the boundaries of law. In these countries we've seen two phenomena become more pronounced: on the one hand, an interpretation of law in terms of the rights granted to a multiplicity of groups as such; on the other, legislative practices aimed at putting the letter of the law everywhere in harmony with new lifestyles, new forms of work, of technology, of family or of social relationships. In correspondence with this shrinking of political sphere, which is constituted in the interval between the law's abstract literalness and the polemics over its interpretations. The law thus celebrated increasingly tends to be the registering of a community's lifestyles. A political symbolization of power, its limits and the ambiguities of law has been replaced by an ethical symbolization of the latter: a relation of consensual inter-expression between the fact of the state of a society and the norm of the law.

The American response affirms this immediate adequation of right and fact within the life of a community. But the dominant representation of the American Constitution also symbolizes it: it is the ethical identity between a particular lifestyle and a universal system of values. 'Ethos' means dwelling and lifestyle before it does a system of moral values. The recent manifesto issued by American intellectuals in support of George W. Bush's policies highlighted this point well: more than a juridico-political community, the United States are first and foremost a community united by common moral and religious values – an ethical community. The Good that founds the community is therefore the identity between right and fact. And the crime perpetrated against thousands of American lives can be immediately posited as a crime perpetrated against the Empire of Good as such.

But a while ago this rise of ethics to the detriment of justice was already taking shape in the forms of foreign interventions undertaken by the great powers. In them, the blurring of the limits between fact and law has taken another figure, opposite and complementary to that of consensual harmony – the figure of the humanitarian and of 'humanitarian interference'. The 'right of humanitarian interference' has enabled the protection of specific populations of ex-Yugoslavia from an undertaking of ethnic liquidation. But it was done at the price of blurring the borders of the symbolic as well as of the state. Not only did it seal the definitive abandon of a structural principle of international law, namely the principle of non-inference – a principle of admittedly ambiguous virtues; above all, it introduced a principle of limitlessness that ruins the very idea of the gap between right and fact, which grants the law its status.

At the time of the Vietnam War or of the *coups d'état* more or less directly incited by American power in various regions throughout the world, there existed an opposition, more or less explicit, between the great principles asserted by Western powers and the practices subordinating those principles to their vital interests. The anti-imperialist mobilizations of the 1960s–1970s had condemned this gap between founding principles and real practices. Today the polemic over means and ends seems to have vanished. The principle of this disappearance is the representation of the absolute victim, the victim of an infinite evil, obliging infinite reparation. This 'absolute' right of the victim has developed in the framework of 'humanitarian' war. And it has been seconded by the major intellectual movement of theorizing infinite crime, which has been elaborated over the last quarter of a century.

The specificity of what might be called the second denunciation of Soviet crimes and the Nazi genocide has without doubt received too little attention. The first denunciation had aimed to establish the reality of the facts, while also reinforcing the determination of Western democracies to struggle against an ever-present and still-threatening totalitarianism. The second, developed during the 1970s as a ledger of communism or in the 1980s by way of a return to the extermination of the European Jewry, has acquired a wholly new meaning. These crimes have not only been construed as the monstrous effects of regimes that have to be fought against, but as the forms of manifestation of an infinite crime, unthinkable and irreparable, as the work of an Evil power exceeding all legal and political measure. Ethics has become the way of thinking about this infinite evil, creating an irremediable cut in history.

The ultimate consequence of the excess of ethics over law and politics is the paradoxical constitution of an absolute right for those whose rights have been absolutely denied. This figure in effect appears as the victim of an infinite Evil against which the fight is itself infinite. So the defender of the victim's right gets to inherit this absolute right. The limitlessness of the irreparable wrong perpetrated against the victim then justifies the unlimited right of his defender. American reparation for the absolute crime committed against American lives brought the process to its point of culmination. The obligation of attending to the victims of absolute Evil is identified with the limitless fight against this evil. And this is identified with the deployment of exorbitant military might, functioning like a police force in charge of restoring order to every part of the world where Evil can find shelter. But this military power is also a juridical power, carrying out against all the supposed accomplices of infinite Evil the mythical power of Vengeance tracking down the Crime.

As the adage has it, unlimited right is identical with non-right. Victims and culprits alike fall into the circle of 'infinite justice' which today results in the total legal indeterminacy affecting the status of prisoners of the US Army and the qualification of the facts held against them. Long ago Hegel mocked the night of the Absolute in which 'all cows are grey'. The indistinctness of ethics, in which politics and the law are smothered today, has turned the prisoners of Guantanamo Bay into captives of an Infinite of like genre, which has simply traded grey for orange.

The ethico-police symbolization of the lives of so-called democratic communities and of their relations with another world – which is likened to the sole reign of ethnic and fundamentalist powers – has slowly come to replace juridico-political forms of symbolization. On one side, the world of good: that of consensus eliminating political litigation in the felicitous harmonization of right and fact, of ways of being and values; on the other, the world of evil, in which wrong is, on the contrary, infinitized and where it can only be played out as a war unto death.

CHAPTER TWENTY-TWO
From One Month of May to Another, *June 2002*

Between the end of April and the start of May, the streets of Paris and of many other towns in France were filled with corteges of demonstrators and notably of crowds of youths in a way not seen since the month of May 1968. However, one difference separated these two Springs: in 1968, the demonstrators had noisily contrasted the reality of political and social power that they represented to the electoral games of the parties. Their disinterest for the elections then organized by the Général de Gaulle found expression in the slogan: 'Elections, idiot trap'. In 2002, the slogan born by those who had not entered the street since 1968 and the youths who were marching in them for the first time was, conversely: 'Abstention, idiot trap'. It was as if this street movement's foremost task was to atone for a good 30 years of sin.

This was perhaps the most profound sense of the events surrounding the French presidential election. Regardless of what was said about it, the most important aspect was not the result obtained by the extreme-right. This result was perhaps slightly above its average of the last 15 years, but was by no means tsunami-like. Moreover, it expressed a force that was closer to a diffuse movement of opinion than to a fascist party on the verge of taking power. This slight increase became a traumatic event, however, because the mechanism of the majority-rules system, designed to secure the two governmental parties a monopoly in the struggle for power, for once resulted in the contrary. The Socialist Party had broadly benefited from the electoral strength of the extreme-right and the fact that it took votes away from the official right. This time the mechanism turned against it.

But if the socialist representative could be eliminated from the second round by the extreme-right, this is obviously for another reason. It is because the 'left' votes that it usually depends on were lacking. Here, again, the majority-rules mechanism began to function in reverse. For 20 years the official left had been able to obtain, retain or regain power thanks to the votes of the other left, namely the left that lays claim to the heritage of the 68 years, that fought in the social movement of 1995, and that, in subsequent years, has mobilized against racist laws, against capitalist globalization or for the regularization of workers without papers. The official left has generally benefited from the votes of this militant left, which is more interested in the development of political movements of struggle than in electoral processes. As it has reckoned that it is at any rate guaranteed these votes, the official left has never been bothered to earn them. In particular, it has done nothing to provide a political solution to the problem of integrating workers of foreign origin and their children. For 20 years, it has done nothing but continue to delay making good on its promise, albeit a rather modest one: the participation of foreigners in local elections. The French, they have said, are not yet ready to take this step. As if the average voter was really too backwards to accept the absolutely incredible idea according to which it is right that those who live and work in a place are also able to participate in the discussions and decisions that affect the life of this place. These 'not-yet-ready' Frenchmen and women are simply the voters of the opposing party, whom the socialist governors aim to seduce by manifesting their spirit of responsibility. Such, in fact, is the logic of the majority-rules system: the parties of power concern themselves not with addressing the commitments to their voters, who they think will be compelled to vote for them in any case, but with trying to pick up – from among the voters of the opposing party – the little bit extra that secures victory.

The real event of the presidential election is that this logic failed. For the first time since 1968, the militant left refused, in large numbers, to vote for the official left. Of course, this same militant left was the first to be shocked by the result of this breakdown and to fill the streets, alongside the high school students, and express its absolute rejection of the ideas and values of the racist and xenophobic extreme-right that, thanks to the failure of the official left, had qualified for second round of the election. But next there came about a strange reversal of things. The official left, its press and its intellectuals belaboured the demonstrators in the following terms: why are you in the streets today, if not because of a situation for which you are largely responsible? If you had voted like responsible voters for the socialist candidate, nothing like this would have happened. But you preferred to take refuge in abstention or to scatter your votes among protest candidates.

This notion of 'protest' merits our attention. All the authorized analysts explained to us at length that there were two types of candidates for this election: government candidates and protest candidates. But what distinguishes a government candidate from a protest candidate? It is, quite simply, the fact that one is already used to governing and the other is not. The argument says, in a nutshell, that the existing authorities must be returned to power, which is to say that power is the preserve of the two large consensual parties that share in it by means of alternation. That fine logic is disrupted by the fact of 'protestors'. What is a protestor? It could be advanced that protestors are very simply those who remain unsatisfied with the reduction of politics to the art of seizing and maintaining power and that even the success of the extreme-right lies in the fact that it calls for clear-cut collective decisions to be made on the major national and international questions.

This explanation, we know, does not at all appeal to the 'government candidates', nor to any of the journalists, political scientists, sociologists or other intellectuals assigned to explain the former's lack of success. For them, 'to protest' – that is, not to give credence to the consensual parties – is an illness. And for those who represent the adult science of government, there are two major forms of illness: old age and youth. They distinguish the protestors as follows: on the one hand, there are the 'victims of modernity', those that have failed to adapt to the new economic and technological conditions or lifestyles, and that therefore vote for the old-fashioned values of the extreme-right; on the other, there are the eternal children who dream of radical political and social change, and who refuse to support modern, liberal and responsible socialism.

Illnesses are the business of doctors. For those who suffer senility, measures are proposed to help them live better with their situations, in hoping that the march of modernity will push them gently into the grave. For those who suffer juvenility, by contrast, shock treatment is required. They must be made to understand once and for all what politics is. For they imagine that politics consists in fighting for a certain idea of the community, in putting their confidence in the power of intelligence and action of the largest number. They must be cured of this folly, taught to doubt radically this collective capacity and their own ability to judge and act according to their judgement. They must be taught not only that politics for them must consist solely in voting, but also in voting against their choice. He who votes, in effect, always tends to do so according to the ideas that he reckons are just and for the candidates that he thinks are closest to these ideas. That, again, is tantamount to irresponsibility. The irresponsible must be taught to understand that the principle of the vote is not about choice but submission, not about confidence but fear. This is by and large what Hobbes said when he made fear the principle of the community founded on unconditional submission to the sovereign power. The big names of the official left have transformed Hobbesian theory into a practical exercise of mortification: you did not want to vote for the candidate of the official and responsible left. You should atone. And how to atone, if not by voting overwhelmingly at the second round for the man who represents the current system of government in its most mediocre and most corrupt aspects, by voting, that is purely and simply for submission to the sovereign – a submission whose exemplarity increases in accordance with the contemptibility of the person who embodies this sovereign?

How does the mechanism of submission work? By playing on the double source of guilt and fear. By producing fear by means of guilt and guilt by means of fear. The task was not an easy one, as the polls conducted the evening before the first round predicted Chirac's overwhelming victory in the second. In the days following it, then, we saw develop, in the press and the artistic and intellectual leftist milieus, an intense alarmist campaign, talking up the pseudo-polls of the secrets services that revealed incredible levels of support for Le Pen. Preaching campaigns then sprang up, often run by figures more or less emblematic of the 68 years, trying to convince us all that, if we abstained from putting a vote in the ballot box for Chirac, we would become the witting accomplices of the imminent opening of concentration camps in France.

We then beheld hundreds of thousands of demonstrators turn their own power against themselves. They had filled the streets to express their dismay and their refusal against the extraordinary publicity that the official left's failure had served up to the candidate of a racist France. They were obliged to defile under the banners of contrition and fear, sporting their placards which said: 'Vote the crook, not the fascist'. Or again: 'Better a Banana Republic than a Hitlerite France'. As no one could seriously believe in the threat of a Hitlerite France, the directive in fact meant: better a banana republic than the Republic that all of us gathered here could imagine building with our own forces. Better a banana republic, that is to say, in general, submission.

We know that this campaign was an overnight success. It assured the electoral success of the politician who epitomized submission by fear. By the same token, it provided an irrefutable verification of the argument which seals the success of the extreme-right, namely that it is the only force opposed to the consensus, the only force, that is, to be actually engaged in doing politics. As for the long-term effects of this twofold demonstration, it does not appear that the campaign's promoters have paid much heed to them.

CHAPTER TWENTY-THREE
Victor Hugo: The Ambiguities of a Bicentenary,
August 2002

So, Victor Hugo was born 200 years ago. Anniversaries do not depend on men's wills. It is otherwise for celebrations. Two years ago, there was no decisive reason to turn the twentieth anniversary of Jean-Paul Sartre's death into an event. But there was a will to signify, through his 'rehabilitation', that a certain page had been turned. As Marxism and the revolution to which he had associated his speech and action, to the scandal of honest people and many of his colleagues, was no longer to be feared, he could be dissociated from it and, on the contrary, his independence as artist and his exigencies as a moralist could be highlighted – features that had always distinguished him from the forces of evil even when he had seemed closest to them. He could thus be integrated into a national tradition of the honest writer, a man, a lover of art and also someone who was mindful of common justice and goods, in contrast to the blindness of scholars seduced by the sirens of theory and totalitarian practice.

For Victor Hugo the procedure is apparently simpler. The celebration of the author of *Les Misérables* seems naturally consistent with a political situation in which the new French government has adopted as its watchword concern for the lowly France: a wording elastic enough to unite the inhabitant of the suburbs caught in delinquency, the *artisan boulanger*, the old-style baker of bread, the small businessman and the local notable. Jean Valjean was a bread thief rather than a baker, but also, once out of prison, a businessman and the mayor of an industrial town. But above all this celebration of Victor Hugo is part of the great undertaking to oppose the bad tradition of yesterday's intellectual, the immoral idoliser of the necessities of the dialectic and the ruses of history, with the good tradition of the day before yesterday's intellectual, the moralist, lover of justice, social justice and public instruction.

For a long time these nineteenth-century republicans, lovers of human fraternity and progress of the people through instruction, were the object of an ambiguous tribute, which was readily mixed with suspicion and mockery. Marxists mocked the sentimental republicans and socialists, who dissimulated the naked realities of class struggle behind grand words and believed they could cure social evils with generous sentiments and public instruction. But the anti-Marxists bore just as much of a grudge against them: did not the bombast with which they denounced misery create a sentimental atmosphere of compassion for the humble opening of the door to murderous egalitarian illusions and encourage the complacency of intellectuals towards totalitarianisms? Did not their calls to universal fraternity contribute to disarming the will of democracies in confronting their adversaries? So long as there was fear of the spectre of communism, the phantoms of the great fraternal and humanitarian faith were themselves suspect. The morality of idealists was thought of as an accomplice to the brutality of realist revolutionaries. This point already found ironical expression in Gavroche's song from *Les Misérables*:

I have fallen to earth
Tis the fault of Voltaire
With my nose in the gutter,
Tis the fault of Rousseau![1]

Now that the fear of communism is distanced, history can be rewritten and re-evaluated. Morality, for a long time associated with the facile flight from realities and a dubious complacency towards revolutionary illusions, today is the principle that governors, warlords and ideologues claim informs all their action. So, now, Voltaire and Rousseau, Hugo, Michelet or Zola are able to furnish the example of good intellectuals, those who denounced the real abuses of their times and defended the essential values of civilization and the community. In this vein, part of the French intellectual class sings the praises of these national heroes of universal thought, as opposed to the miserable petty intellectuals of the twentieth century: receivers of salaries or subsidies from democratic governments, who fiercely deny the liberty they thus enjoy, and sing the praises of totalitarianism.

On top of these *post mortem* triumphs is added, it is true, a half-mock half-serious worry. Those who, 10 years ago, celebrated the final victory of liberal democracy, human rights and the individual over the constraints or the horrors of collectivism, now change their tone. Today, they say, there are too many rights and too few duties, too much free individual choice and too little collective discipline and social bond. Democratic individualism now supposedly imperils democracy itself. Against this, the reported remedy is to revitalize the great tradition of educative republicanism, teaching all and sundry to how to put their own private demands second to the great universalist values and the sense of the common bond. The moment is one of return to the founding fathers of civic life, whether their name is Thomas Jefferson or Victor Hugo. Nostalgics for social movements, naturally, have a more caustic interpretation of this return to the great figures of republican idealism. If *Les Misérables* is in the news again, it is because misery is also in the news, because the neo-liberal destruction of the forms of protection and social solidarity have again turned it into an individual matter, an object of the solicitude of social surveyors, of philanthropic associations and of big-hearted men of letters.

To both these groups, however, it is possible to show that this big heart has its ambiguities and this is precisely what forms the actuality of the poet. Victor Hugo presented *Les Misérables* as a great cry directed against the 'degradation of man by the proletariat'. But this cry is far from being univocal. Not only because he divides misery into two: into a problem to resolve by the governments of men and a mystery confided to divine providence. But above all, because compassion for the victims of the social order is mixed with a singular fascination of the obscure dregs of this order. As lyrical as the description of heroic death of republicans on the barricades is, we sense that the poet is more interested by the episode that follows where Jean Valjean caves in as he carries the body of the wounded Marius into the 'intestine of Leviathan', that is to say into the great Parisian sewer. The obscure underneath of the brilliant city is, for politicians, a world that blames the social order for its misery or a realm of subversion that undermines this order's bases. For the novelist, the 'descent into the underworld' of society is something else: a dive into this underground world which is the secret truth of the other, into the universe of the great equality which supports the surface of social distinctions and takes in its old rags. The sewer is, he says, the 'city's consciousness', the 'great cynic' who says all: the judge's hat wallowing beside a rotten part that was once the servant's skirt, the *louis d'or* mingling with the nail of the suicide victim, or this *fin de marquise* bed linen which is now the shroud of a revolutionary.

This great pell-mell is something other than an aesthete's curiosity. It is the emblem of another equality than that for which the insurgents fight. It is also the emblem of a new idea of art. For a long time art had decorated palaces and served to fête the great of this world. During Hugo's time, art began to dedicate itself to a new beauty: not that of the exploits of the people, but that of the unprecedented splendour which arises out of the very fall of former grandeurs. From now on, not only it is that, as Flaubert put it, there is no longer any distinction between noble subjects and vile subjects and that a small Normand provincial town is equal to Constantinople. Rather it is that, at the very moment when some announce the death of art anaesthetized by the grey rationality of the bourgeois order, art discovers a new, endlessly renewable territory: the territory of all the finery of grandeur or opulence of commodities fallen from their social usage and thereby endowed with an unprecedented beauty formed by contradictory elements: they are at once written signs ciphering a history, emblems of the melancholy of disaffected things and testimonies of the naked splendour of what is there without a why, like the rose of the mystic.

Certainly, Hugo only lets himself go halfway towards the charm of this beauty. The chapters of *Les Misérables* about these dregs verge on schizophrenia. The poet sumptuously describes the fantastic landscapes of the sewers; the reformer interrupts him to demand that the fields be fertilized with these excrements thrown unprofitably into the river waters. The former lets himself be fascinated by the monstrous creations of this *langue crapaude* that is slang. The latter stops him to call the governors to spread in torrents the wisdom of instruction which dissipates the darknesses of crime and of its language. Posterity, as for it, has followed the path of this descent into society's unconscious, with greater frankness, in order to exploit the seam of this new beauty of disused things. Surrealist poetics was nourished on it: the promenades by Aragon's *Paysan de Paris* in those old-fashioned Parisian arcades, which are like the opening of the underworld in the heart of the great modern city; photography by Brassaï of the new rock paintings that are wall graffiti or of involuntary sculptures made, for example, of a rolled up bus ticket; shots by Eli Lotar of the Abattoirs; Walter Benjamin's theorization on the 'work of the dia-lectic' within the old-fashioned architecture of disused, nineteenth-century commodity temples. In his recent book titled *Ninfa moderna,* Georges Didi-Huberman attempts to trace the passage from the fallen drapery of the antique sculpture to the displays of clothing by Christian Boltanski or to Steve McQueen's photographs of rolls of carpet in the Parisian gutters. He sees Hugo's sewers and his rags rendered to the mud as a key moment of this evolution, between the ancient beauty of pure lines and noble attitudes and this contemporary beauty, liable to mani-fest itself in a pile of disaffected rags. His argument is open to discussion, but it can be reasonably considered that this heritage of the author of *Les Misérables* is more actual and more profound than the other.

CHAPTER TWENTY-FOUR
The Machine and the Foetus, *January 2003*

When intellectuals no longer really know where they are at, often it happens that artists indicate it to them. This is not because artists have a superior gift of divination. It is simply because it is easier to mark the hour of time when one is not responsible for predicting it or drawing lessons from it. In these times, Parisian intellectuals are lost in an obscure quarrel in which they accuse each other, on the front pages of the main daily newspapers, of having wed the reactionary cause by betraying the ideals of liberty or of equality or both at the same time, without us having any clear idea of what these belligerents are talking about.[1] Conversely, the visitor who steps through the door of the *Musée d'Art moderne de la Ville de Paris*, where there is a retrospective of Picabia's works and a presentation of Matthew Barney's *Cremaster* cycle, has the rather mind-blowing feeling of completely understanding in 2 hours both the ideals of a century and their transformations.

The Picabia exhibition, for starters, takes the figure of the encyclopae-dia. The first painting that it presents is a Pissarro truer than nature, while the last ones, painted in the 1950s–1960s, are part of the informal painting movement. In between time, the painter will have painted the most resolutely cubist paintings, works emblematic of dadaism and the most convincing testimonies of the return to a most academic sort of realism. Owing to his date of birth, he will only have avoided the oldest of the schools that stamped the three-quarters of a century that he traversed. Symbolism alone is missing from the collection of styles from which he borrowed. Now, this is the missing link that is presented, in its most radical form, in the *Cremaster* cycle. Through the analogies that it composes between musical films, plastic sculptures and Cibachrome, it replays the Wagnerian dream of the total work of art. It also shows off all the imagery and the favourite procedures of an era: scenery of glaciers or of Rococo colonnades, smooth forms and undulating lines, art-deco aesthetics turning a car shell or a table service into absolute poems, variations of post-romantic opera set against *fin-de-siècle* gilt, aquatic divinities, nymphs, satyrs and ballets with young girls or evocations of Celtic legends.

The relation between these two floors of the *Musée d'Art Moderne* thus composes a singular dramaturgy of modern art. In Matthew Barney's work can be seen the last episode of the legend of a century, simply leaping the pop and conceptual ages and sublimating the neo-Gothic bric-à-brac of contemporary forms of music or films to return one cycle of art to its point of departure. Conversely, it can be said that the *Cremaster* cycle recapitulates the whole symbolist, spiritualist, Wagnerian and aesthetizing hotchpotch against which, in the 1910s, the futurist or dadaist provocations were mounted by young people such as Picabia, in considering that, if that was art, then it would be better to put it to death and celebrate the joyous reign of the machine.

To be retained, then, more than the traversing of the forms of a century, is the opposition of two characteristic moments: the 1910s/1920s against the 1990s/2000s. This opposition, however, cannot be reduced to some opposition between a modernist age of radical ruptures and a postmodern age of recuperation and generalized recycling. More complex is the way that their aesthetic paradigms contrast with one another, paradigms which are more broadly about the relation of men with materiality, harbouring antagonistic visions of history and the common world.

With the radical artist of the 1920s and the feted artist of the year 2000, two ideas of anti-nature go head-to-head: machine or artifice. In the years from 1915 to the 1920s, Picabia painted his 'mecanomorphic' paintings. Rejecting traditional pictorial resemblance, he was very faithfully inspired by drawings of machines in scientific journals, if only to give them names of fantasy: *Le Saint des saints* or *Portrait d'une jeune fille américaine dans l'état de nudité*. Later on, he decided to choose the Ripolin-brand enamel used by industrial painters for his paintings. He contrasted, then, the natural order commanded by the tradition of painting to the hardness of metal and the geometry of the machine. This aesthetic choice agrees with a time when great hopes were placed in the machine that would destroy Old Man and promote a new world. Picabia was not much concerned with politics, and even less with revolution. But the link between the inventions of artists and the struggles and hopes of a time passes less through their personal involvements than through a common attitude with regard to the potentials of sensory matter.

Matthew Barney's anti-nature goes by the name of artifice. Its matter is not the metal of dadaist dream machines or of the Soviet epic, but the soft matter of oil derivatives. Nylon, plastic, vinyl and resin are, along with tapioca, the essential primary matter of the more or less monumental sculptures which sometimes serve as replicas, sometimes as pedestals for the images of his films. His cars have neither piston rods nor cylinders, only shells set in moulded plastic. The inventors of the 1920s contrasted the hardness of the machine's gears to the old-world feebleness and the embellishments of the Modern Style. As for Barney, he chose a residual and malleable matter, a matter that is obedient to dreams and to hands alike, preferred by an age which thinks less of changing life than of abolishing the borders separating the living from the non-living.

A 'matter' is always a certain idea of what it is that matter can do for man and of what man can do upon matter. The irony contained in Picabia's mecanomorphic paintings is pretty far removed from futurist euphoria and constructivist dreams. Even so, it is thereby only better able to express what is foremost at stake in them. Let us look again at the titles of these paintings of gears, pistons and pulleys: *Parade d'amour, Le Fiancé* and above all that, reprised several times, *Voilà la fille née sans mère.* The machine's dream is exactly that: the dream of abolished maternal affiliation. This is why it agrees so well with the dream of workers' self-emancipation. The dream of autonomy is that of a male humanity spawning itself. Celibate machines of mischievous artists and the tempered steel of Soviet constructors both cling to the dream of an absolute power of self-engendering. There are, to be sure, many different ways of converting it. With Picabia this capacity is ultimately realized, far from any collective constructivist programme, in the simple virtuosity of the technician who is equally able to make whatever is possible, like canvasses or anti-canvasses, figurations or anti-figurations. It is common to contrast the individualism of artistic invention to the rigour of the collective enterprise. Yet both draw from the same common source. An individualism is always the other face of a collectivism.

There are different ways to liquidate this promethean dream of the man who wants to be his own progenitor. There is the old tragic wisdom which says that the greatest good for mankind would be never to have been born, and that the second greatest would be to die the earliest possible. This wisdom transformed, during the Romantic era, into a nostalgia of the time before birth. Nietzsche summed up the tragic Wagnerian wisdom in Isolde's dying wish, that of losing oneself again in the great original sea of the Indifferentiated. Psychoanalysis, for its part, readily contrasted the communist utopia of the self-creating man to the irreducible misery of the human animal as incomplete animal, marked by the prematuration of its birth. Under its appearances of a return to simple reason, contemporary capitalism perhaps nourishes its own utopia: the utopia of a life escaping from this 'misery', a painless life of consumption, wholly spent in the tranquillity of the maternal womb. The *Cremaster* cycle proposes to retrace, in analogy, the history of the foetus between indifferentiation and sexual differentiation. But this is not merely a matter of analogy or of symbols. The car interiors which Matthew Barney encloses in plastic blocks, evoking at once the protective fat and the purity of glaciers, are clearly illustrative of the overturning of an ideology of metallics and mechanics. The soft matter of artifice is that matter that is always ready to melt into a primitive ocean or into an amniotic liquid to celebrate a foetal life elevated to the dimension of eternity.

Here again the individual and the collective are no more separate than art and politics. Some serious thinkers are regularly perturbed by the dangers that the exacerbated narcissism of 'democratic individualism' presents to the administering of collective interests. But these feigned oppositions may well be no more than two sides of the same coin. The dream of uninterrupted maternal protection expressed by the liquid universe of the fashionable artist is synchronous with this promise of security in which the rich states today symbolize politics as such.

CHAPTER TWENTY-FIVE
The Death of the Author or the Life of the Artist?
April 2003

This time, the author was supposedly really dead. Already 30 years ago, the philosophers reportedly proclaimed his theoretical death sentence by undermining the foundations of his pretension – the subject as master and possessor of his thoughts. This was the epoch when pop artists, with their portraits of stars or their series of soup tins, would destroy the privilege of the unique oeuvre. Following afterward were such things as: an art of installations in which the artist often remained content to rearrange objects of use and already existing images; the practice of DJs mixing sonorous elements borrowed from existing compositions to the point of rendering them unrecognisable; and, lastly, the information revolution, instituting the uncontrolled reproducibility of texts, songs and images.

What thus appeared to come undone was the very content which constituted the notion of the work: the expression of the creative will of an author in a specific material that he had worked over, singularized in the figure of the work, posited as an original distinct from all its reproductions. The idea of the work became radically independent of any work done on a particular material. Bertrand Lavier's *Salle des Martin* exhibited 50 paintings painted by authors bearing the name of Martin. None of these paintings any longer played the role of the original work. The work's originality here passes over into the idea, in itself immaterial, of their gathering. Any old heap of materials can then stand in for the work, such as this pile of old papers here, the element of a Damien Hirst installation that an employee of a Londonian Museum, in the concerns of cleanliness, ill-advisedly threw in the bin.

It is tempting to liken this indistinctiveness which renders all material indifferent to that which transforms discourses, images or music into bits of information. With the information revolution, all materiality, it is said, is transformed into an ideality. Ideas, images and music, likewise digitalized, run freely from screen to screen, mocking those who want to claim property rights over them. So the very principle of the author's privilege would seem to have vanished: the difference between the means of creation and the machines of reproduction. Some see in this the power of the brain-world or of the machine-world that causes ownership and domination to shatter. The proletarians of all countries are not united to bury bourgeois domination, but the technical revolution has supposedly confirmed, to the detriment of intellectual and artistic property, the other great prophecy of the *Communist Manifesto*: 'All that is solid melts into air'. Taking over where the faltering producers left off, the machines of reproduction work towards a new communism, rendering all reality immaterial, and therefore inappropriable.

This faith in the communist virtues of technology is not without problems. Neither the engineers nor the jurists are short on ways to reformulate property rights and invent software programmes to make sure that they are respected. But above all, technical reproducibility has no obvious consequence on the conceptual status of the author. In the 1930s Walter Benjamin had seen in the industrial conditions of reproduction and cinematographic dissemination the principle of an art liberated from the *aura* of the unique work. The prophecy was not born out: at the very moment when Broodthaers, Beuys and the Fluxus artists made a mockery of museum art, the young Turks of the *Cahiers du cinéma* enshrined the 'politics of the author'. And just as museums converted to the prose of installations, Jean-Luc Godard's *Histoire(s) du Cinéma* adopted the sacredness of Malraux's imaginary Museum. Despite the multitude of constraints that a film places on production and on artistic and technical collaborations, the cinematic 'director' has become the exemplary embodiment of the author who puts his stamp on his creation.

But no doubt the excessive confidence placed in the effect of the technological revolution followed from a somewhat simplistic view of the author. A received opinion has it that artistic and literary modernity since romanticism has been linked with the development of the cult of the author, born at the same time as the rights of the same name and as the individualism of the 'bourgeois revolution'. In consequence, anything that contradicts this privilege – from series of images of stars or of commercial products of the pop age to the piracies of the digital age – is attributed to a postmodern revolution, which is reported to have destroyed, if not the legal property rights, at least the modernist illusions of artistic originality associated with the myth of the owner-author.

But the relations between the author, the owner and the person are infinitely more complex. The enshrining of the literary genius did not arise at the end of the eighteenth century with Beaumarchais' acts in favour of authorial rights nor with the offensives of bourgeois individualism. It arose, on the contrary, with the fury of the epoch's philologists wanting to dispossess Homer of the paternity of his work, and to make it into the anonymous expression of a people and an age. The modern idea of the author was born at the same time as that of the impersonality of art. This equivalence between the author and the anonymous force passing through it was given expression in the concept of the genius during the Romantic era. And the supposed representatives of art for art's sake and of the cult of artists has never ceased, with Flaubert, to voice the radical impersonality of art or, with Mallarmé, to affirm that the poet was necessarily 'dead as so-and-so'.

This idea has never prevented any artist from claiming his authorial rights. But it defined a splitting of the idea of property, a singular link between propriety and impropriety. Nearly two centuries before Sherry Levine made a work in photographing the photographs of Walker Evans, the Schlegel Brothers re-poetized classical poems by updating them to the times of romantic poets. Meanwhile, the surrealists showed that the most personal expressions of the absolute of desire and of dream could coincide with the recycling of out-of-use commodities or of old-fashioned illustrations of magazines and catalogues. The absolute and impersonal author is the one that has a patrimony of art at his disposition, which can be extended to any object whatsoever.

Thereby is a solidarity affirmed between the impersonality of the artistic process and the indifference of its subjects, which is borrowed from the impersonality of ordinary life. Walter Benjamin showed how photography had become an art by renouncing the composition of the canvass to appropriate the image of the anonymous. The photography of the small fisheress of New Haven, he said, had done more for the glory of David Octavius Hill than his great pictorial compositions. Photography thus set itself up in the wake of the literary revolution which had assimilated, with Flaubert, the absolute of a book held solely by its style with the harnessed impersonality of language, of dreams, and of the lives of nondescript individuals. The cult of art is born with the affirmation of the splendour of the anonymous.

In one sense, we can say that the performances and installations of contemporary art carry to its ultimate consequence the impersonality of creation and the indifference of its material. Sophie Calle's 'stolen' images in hotel rooms would thus be the contemporary version of the *Journal d'une femme de chambre* and, more broadly, of the romantic dream of entering into the life of absolutely anyone. But perhaps this apparent consequence conceals a logical reversal which overturns the notion of the author otherwise than this is habitually described: not in making it disappear in the banality of things and the infinity of reproductions but, on the contrary, in likening it to the personal ownership of the idea. The Flaubertian idea of the absolute work compelled the novelist to identify the splendours of his phrase with the reproduction of the banality of the world. The Idea of the contemporary artist, on the contrary, is withdrawn, hovering in survey over the work of its realization. Christian Boltanski himself had no need to affix on the wall the anonymous photographs which line the halls of exhibitions. And Lawrence Weiner had no need to take his rifle to pierce a miniscule hole in the museum wall which constitutes his quasi-immaterial contribution to a recent exhibition.

What gets lost, then, is neither the author's personality nor the work's materiality. It is the work by which this personality is supposedly altered in this materiality. The work's retreat into the idea does not annul the material reality of the work. But it tends to transform the paradoxical property of the impersonal work into the logical property of an inventor's patent. The contemporary author is, in this sense, more strictly a property holder than any author has ever been. The pact is thus broken between the impersonality of art and that of its material. While the former is closer to the property of the idea, the latter tends to be displaced towards the property of the image.

Generations of photographers have made art in capturing, in the streets of great metropolises, fetes of the suburbs or popular beaches, everyday occupations or the extraordinary pleasures of the anonymous. Today these anonymous individuals are called upon to make themselves recognized, to reclaim, instead of the immortalization of art, more tangible rights over the property of the image that has been stolen from them. Property does not dissolve itself in the immateriality of the network. On the contrary, it tends to stamp with its seal all that is apt to enter the sphere of art, to make art into a negotiation between owners of ideas and owners of images.

This is doubtless the reason that autobiography, which makes both properties coincide, takes up so much place in the art of our time. We think of those writers who publish only the interminable journal of their life and their thoughts; of those photographers who privilege their own image, such as Cindy Sherman, or the scenes of intimacy between close relations, such as Nan Goldin; of those directors who, like Nanni Moretti, compress their work on the epoch around the chronicle of their lives; of those artists-installers who, like Mike Kelley or Annette Messager, populate their works with the soft toys of their fantasies rather than with hijacked objects or images of the world.

Today the author *par excellence* is supposedly the one who exploits what already belongs to him, his own image. The author is then no longer the 'spiritual histrion' of which Mallarmé spoke, but the comedian of his image. The art of the comedian always tends towards a limit which is the transformation of the simulacrum into reality. Working on the physical remodelling of her face, Orlan is thus, in this sense, the typical artist of our time. At the hour of universal digitalization, the 'death' of which Mallarmé spoke still seems rather alive. A little too alive, indeed.

CHAPTER TWENTY-SIX
The Logic of Amnesia, *June 2003*

'My memory's giving out' – thus begins the song that serves as the emblem of Francois Truffaut's *Jules et Jim*.[1] What the heroine could not recall very well was the beloved's name and eye colour: 'Were they blue? Were they grey? . . . His name was, we called him . . . What was his name?'

Forgetting the sensory qualities of a being external to oneself generally passes as a benign form of memory trouble. And the emotion of love is commonly associated with the impossibility of being able to represent adequately its cause. Clearly more serious is the fact of not remembering at the end of a sentence what one wanted to say in beginning it, or of forgetting at the port of arrival, the reasons for which one left on voyage. Still more serious is the fact of forgetting in succession what one has said and done.

This amnesia is at the heart of our actuality. Throughout the year, day after day, 24 hours a day, George Bush and his advisors, republicans and democrats and a cohort of journalists, experts and councillors in all things, have gone untrammelled, one after the other, on the screens of CNN, Fox and so on to express the terror that they felt and that we should all feel because of the weapons of mass destruction that are in the possession of the Iraqi leader. However, the closer that the armies, sent to incapacitate the possessor of these weapons, were to reaching their goal, the more this goal seemed to fade from memory. As the troops passed through, no weapons of mass destruction were encountered: there was therefore no time to speak – on the same channels, which were busy with narrating hour by hour what was happening – about the non-information constituted by this non-encounter.

Such is precisely that in which continuous information consists: it only speaks about what it is that makes up information: the felt threat, expressed 24 hours a day; the intervention that responds to the threat. Where can we find the time to recall the cause of the threat and to ask whether the intervention has verified it? Where is the time left for surprise about the fact that he who possesses the weapons of mass destruction forgets to use them or gets busy hiding them when he is attacked?

Some people could respond that the hypothetical possession of weapons of mass destruction was a secondary issue as compared to an absolutely certain reality: that Iraq was governed by a dictator. The intervention found its ultimate legitimacy less in the neutralization of the dictator's weapons than in the gift given to his people of the contrary of dictatorship, called democracy or liberty.

There is not much difficultly in having the idea acknowledged that freedom is preferable to dictatorship. The difficulty lies in knowing what this freedom consists in and to whom it falls to prefer it to servitude. One who takes the trouble to bring freedom to others must suppose that it is a positive good whose power alone dissipates the darknesses of the 'axis of evil'. However, when interrogated over what he thought about the pillages in Baghdad, the American minister of defence, who was the brains behind operation *Iraqi Freedom,* responded singularly as follows: freedom is indivisible, it is therefore also the freedom to commit faults and crimes.

The problem is that the Iraqis never lacked this latter freedom, nor did others, and that on this count the dictator, too, was as free to commit crimes or possess weapons of mass destruction as the pillagers were to strip his palaces bare. This gift of freedom must be understood other than as the free will to choose between good and evil. It must be understood as the positive good that constitutes, for a people, the possibility of self-government. It is this good that the American armies allegedly brought to the Iraqi people in ridding them of their dictator. Of course, to do this it was necessary to cast definitively aside the rule of international law that prohibits one state from meddling in the domestic affairs of another. This barrier was at first only timidly pulled down in the form of the 'right to humanitarian interference'. This right, initially claimed by humanitarian organizations to save populations in danger of extermination, was taken up from them, at the charge, by the great powers. A superior right was thus set over against the traditional rules of international law, namely the absolute right of the victim of absolute wrong. The victim of absolute wrong is the one who has no way at all of asserting his rights. It follows quite obviously that this right which prevails over every rule of law can only be exercised by another, in simple terms by a foreign army of intervention.

How can this right of exception become the rule? For this to occur, the privation of political liberty must itself be identified with the situation of absolute distress which justifies the intervention of the righter of wrongs. Now, the sufferance of being deprived of political liberty is more difficult to verify than that of being thrown into the streets after having seen one's house burnt down and family exterminated. Unless one makes an argument of the very absence of suffering to identify both situations and legitimate the intervention. So what is, it will be asked, the well-known consequence of dictatorship? It is to take away from the subjugated the taste of freedom, thus the suffering of its privation. The impossibility that they have to demand their freedom is therefore the absolute suffering which makes it incumbent upon others to hand it to them, were it by the force of arms.

The argument here becomes somewhat subtle and, rather than the orators of *Fox News*, it is the philosophers who take on the onus of handling it. On the eve of the conflict, a French philosopher published a chronicle in *Le Monde* in which he got right into those impenitent pacifists who raised the question of whether peoples could, despite themselves, really be given the gift of freedom.[2] Let us not ask peoples what they want, he replied. The response is pretty well known. Even since the year 1576 when Étienne de La Boétie published his *Traité de la servitude volontaire*, we have known that what people want is to be alienated. Little matter by what: consumption, religions, symbols. They have always wanted it and always will. So . . .

So, what? That is the problem. From this affirmation, it is possible to conclude everything – and its contrary. First conclusion: since they want to be alienated, they must be allowed their masters. Second conclusion: they must be liberated despite themselves, though they may use this liberty to alienate themselves anew. Third conclusion: since, in any case, they will be alienated, they must be alienated by better masters, by free masters. It remains of course to know why the people thus burdened with imposing its freedom on others itself escapes the universal preference of peoples for servitude.

In philosophy, this is called an undetermined argument: an argument such that, the premises being posited, any conclusion can be deduced from them. An undetermined finite argument completes the spiral specific to the politics of amnesia. The conqueror forgets what it is that he went to look for. The journalist forgets to ask him if he found it. The politician who exults the freedom brought to the oppressed *manu militari* forgets that he has, over the course of decades, designated the specificity of totalitarianism as a desire to want to give people happiness despite themselves. The philosopher forgets, in the middle of his argument, that nothing can be deduced from it other than the equivalence of all the conclusions.

Our present is readily described as the age of amnesia. Ordinarily, the fault for this is laid on the new technologies of memory and of communication. They say that the television, the Internet and the reign of communication has made us forgetful by imposing on us their limitless present and their reality itself indissociable from simulation. But this amounts to charging technology with more crimes than it can commit. The information machines communicate what their masters make them communicate. The explanation must rather be sought on the side of the masters. It is the absorption of politics in the pure exercise of limitless power which imposes this continuous amnesia and this loss of reason in the indefinite. The logic of global government is that of an indistinction wherein all differences are abolished. For this government's only affair is with an evil posited as infinite and a terror which is without before or afterwards.

Not long ago 'infinite justice' was the name working to enshrine the vanishing of all the distinctions that had hitherto served to delimit justice: private vengeance and public sanction, war and police operation, politics, law, morality and religion, all likewise engulfed in the infinite war of good against evil. The indistinctness of power now extends its reign to the abolition of temporal differences, to the reign of this uninterrupted present where the before and the afterward are no more distinguishable than the cause and the effect or the means and the end.

Formerly it was said that power would always find the facts and the arguments it needed to legitimate itself. Today, it is instead the forgetting of facts and the impossibility of seeing to the end of one's reasoning which accompanies the deployment of superpower. Not simply is it that these things serve its desires better. More radically, it is perhaps because the specific element of limitless power is to remember no longer what it was that it wanted, to destroy the very time in which it might be able to remember.

CHAPTER TWENTY-SEVEN
The Insecurity Principle, *September 2003*

In this summer of 2003, in which the American government has had to confront the unforeseen consequences of its victorious campaign in Iraq, the French government was called to task by another unforeseen enemy, the heatwave, which killed more than ten thousand people in a month. What is the relation between the Iraqi politico-military furnace and the unusual severity of the French summer? That of highlighting the increasingly massive role that the obsession with securitization plays in so-called advanced states.

The stated goal of Iraq campaign was to respond to the threat presented by a rogue state, possessor of weapons of mass destruction able to reach western states in less than an hour. There is little plausibility to the notion that American and British leaders really believed the tall-tale told about this threat, brandished to muster the support of their fellow-citizens for the war. It remains to find out why they needed a war against a danger that they knew not to exist. If the traditional economist explanation that sees some oil-related affair behind every conflict of our time leaves us unsatisfied, then is it perhaps necessary to invert the terms of the problem. If the war was necessary, it was not to respond to a situation, real or imaginary, of insecurity. It was to maintain this sentiment of insecurity, necessary to the good functioning of states.

In view of the most common analyses of the relation between our societies and their governments tell us, this might seem absurd. These analyses are apt to describe contemporary capitalist states as exercising a power that is increasingly diluted and invisible, synchronous with the flows of commodities and of communication. The advanced capitalist state is said to be one of automatic consensus, of painless adjustment between the collective negotiation of power and the individual negotiation of pleasures within mass democratic society. It functions to take the heat out of conflicts and to divest values.

The present uproar over weapons, the renewed hymns to God and the flag, and the revival of some of the grossest state propaganda lies would seem to undermine this dominant view. In those places where the commodity reigns limitlessly, in post-Reagan America and post-Thatcherite England, the form of optimal consensus is not that of the management state; it is that cemented by the fear of a society grouped around the protectionist police state. In denouncing the illusions of consensus, we still conceived of the consensual state in terms of the tradition of the State of arbitration applying itself to minimal forms of wealth redistribution appropriate to maintaining social peace. Now, as the state tends to unburden itself of its functions of social regulation to give free run to the law of Capital, consensus adopts an apparently more archaic face. The consensual state in its accomplished form is not the management state. It is the state reduced to the purity of its essence, that is, the police state. The community of sentiment which supports this state and which this state turns to its advantage – aided by a media which clearly does not have to be owned by the state to support its propaganda – is the community of fear.

The American government's conflict with 'old Europe' consists perhaps in a contrast between two types of consensual state, where the one that is most 'advanced' is not the one we may think. But insecurity is also on the agenda in old Europe, and in forms that are more fragmented, indeed more tortuous, than those of the great crusade against the axis of Evil. As such, the last French presidential election presented a remarkable combat – or a remarkable complicity – between rival forms of insecurity. The discourse proferred by the rightwing candidate about the extreme rightwing candidate was built entirely around the theme of the insecurity caused by immigration. The official right candidate proclaimed that immigration alone was capable of fighting effectively against this insecurity. Lastly, the left rushed to the rescue of the right candidate, holding him up as the last rampart of democracy against the supreme cause of insecurity – the danger of the totalitarian pest.

Since this time, the defence of endangered democracy and the fight against threatening insecurity have tended to become more discreet. The priorities adopted by the French government have concentrated on the 'modernization' of the state and country, that is to say the lightening of the state's social burden. But insecurity is thereby represented with a new face. Over the course of August, the government found itself accused of its lack of foresight, which ended up leaving thousands of old folks to perish as victims of this rare heatwave. The president defended himself meekly and initiated an inquest into the conditions of that negligence, but in so doing he *de facto* confirmed the notion expressed by this opinion, that he ought, if not exactly to make rain and good weather, then at least to predict the consequences of temperature change for diverse categories of the population.

Here again, we are faced with an apparently paradoxical and nevertheless logical situation. Exactly when the government, according to good liberal doctrine, pledges to lower taxes, reduces public spending on health and cuts down on the traditional systems of social protection, it accepts its responsibility for the accidents that might be triggered by climatic changes. Right when the state does less for our health, it decides to do more for our lives.[1]

It is not certain that this change will greatly reduce state spending. What it will do, however, is change the relation between individuals and the state. It was only yesterday that official hymns still sang the benefits of responsibility and of taking individual risks as opposed to the cautious 'privileges' afforded by the systems of social protection. Today it is more than evident that the weakening of systems of social protection also involves establishing a new relation between individuals and a state power that is made accountable for security in general, for all the forms of security against threats that are themselves multiform: terrorism and Islamism, but also the heat and the cold. This French summer will leave us with the abiding feeling that we have still not taken enough precautions against the inherent threat, that is, heat. That is, the feeling that we have not been protected enough against threats and that we need increasingly more protection – against known threats and against those that we haven't even suspected.

The fault that our governments recognize, or are accused of, with respect to the protection of their populations thus plays on its counter-effect. In not protecting us well, governments prove that they are there to protect us more than ever and that more than ever we must pull tight around them. That the American government was unable to protect its population against an extensively premeditated attack proves superlatively that its very mission consists in preventative protection against an invisible and omnipresent threat. To foresee dangers is one thing; to manage the sentiment of insecurity is another, one in which the state will always be more expert, perhaps because it is the very principle of its power. Prevailing opinion has it that the development of security rationales are the defensive reactions occasioned by the dangers that weigh on advanced societies today from the reactive attitudes of disempowered populations, who are being pushed by poverty towards fanaticism and terrorism. But nothing indicates that either the current militaro-police campaigns or security regulations will lead to a reduction in the gap between the rich and the poor said to constitute the permanent threat weighing on advanced countries. If Iran is invaded after Iraq, there will still be nigh on sixty 'rogue states' left that threaten the security of rich countries.

More, for our countries, insecurity is essentially much more than a set of facts. It is a mode of management of collective life. The daily media management of all forms of danger, risk and catastrophe – from terrorisms to heat waves – not to mention the intellectual tsunami of catastrophe discourses and the morality of the lesser evil suffice to show that the theme of insecurity has unlimited resources at its disposal. The declaration of hostility by enlightened opinion against the Iraq campaign perhaps might not have been so vociferous had the operations been aimed at toppling governments in countries whose lack of foresight risked triggering some climatic, ecological, health or other type of catastrophe. The sentiment of insecurity is not an archaic tension that has resulted from circumstances in themselves transitory. It is a mode of management of states and of the planet that is geared towards reproducing and renewing, in circular fashion, the very circumstances that maintain it.

CHAPTER TWENTY-EIGHT
The New Fictions of Evil, *November 2003*

Evil is doing well. In the shadows of the great Bushian *mise-en-scene* of the fight against the axis of the same name, several pieces of fiction have been produced recently that are dedicated to presenting the crusade in its inverted version: showing the way in which this America, as it hunts down death-makers across the entire surface of the globe, finds them again at home, at the heart of the wide maple-lined avenues and the modern and convivial schools of middle America, in the figure of honourable citizens and of adolescents like all others.

Evil is not violence. Violence can be domesticated in various ways. On the one hand, it can be dealt with as a pure intensity: thunderous explosions, streams of blood and buildings collapsing in flames are thus, like deluges of decibels or spectacular camera movements, pure intensities which make up the enjoyment of a spectacle from which one leaves as one entered. From this viewpoint, then, violence has no repercussions. From another, on the contrary, it lends itself to the game of differences and of causes. There is good and bad violence. Not too long ago at the cinema, freelance sheriffs and righters of wrongs used to wield, without inhibition, the violence of the common law, or of morality, against the violence of those who followed the law out of mere greed.

On the world stage, we rediscover, under an elapsed form, an opposition of the same type: as was said in the times of Sartre and Frantz Fanon, there is violence which oppresses and violence which liberates. This difference could be made because it was possible to assign causes to the violence, to refer it back to a more hidden violence, namely the violence of order and property. On this basis, political scenarios were devised about the toughness required for justice, or aesthetic scenarios presenting confrontations between these types of violence.

Today, to all appearances, these scenarios provoke suspicion. Michael Moore's *Bowling for Columbine* attests to this in its own way. The argument according to which 'there are crimes because there are weapons that anyone at all can buy' straddles an awkward position between two different logics. According to the old logic, the causal schema would involve not simply pitting between a lobby group's interests against an American ideal of virility, but the very fact of living in a society in which everything is bought. If Moore stops causal chain where he does, this is of course because it corresponds to the contemporary forms of left consciousness, which are more attached to the regulation of dangerous products than to the critique of property as such. But in addition it leaves the way free for another form of causality, namely that which refers the finite fact of such-and-such a murderous act to the infinite fact of evil.

In effect, the thing about evil is that it cannot be righted except at the price of another evil which remains irreducible. There is a shared trait in three recent films that speak to us of evil in general and of American evil in particular: *Dogville, Mystic River* and *Elephant.* In these films the law is either radically absent (*Elephant*), or else the accomplice of evil: that is, insofar as it designates the victim to suffer and leaves the care of punishing the torturers to the bandits (*Dogville*); or insofar as it leaves unpunished the crime of the honest family father/gangster/righter of wrongs (*Mystic River*). Of these no doubt it is *Dogville* that best shows the gap between the two different logics, which also form a gap between the two eras. Its abstract *mise-en-scene,* which compares the fictive space of the cinema to the real space of the theatre, its composition in small acts, which functions as so many moral tales, and the distancing role of the voice off – all these features recall the theatrical origin of the parable which Lars von Trier proposes to us. The principles of this *mise-en-scene* are inherited from Brecht's 'epic theatre'. And the story of disillusionment endured by the young woman with blue eyes who wants to do good, but is unable to, irrepressibly recalls *Die Heilige Johanne der Schlächthöfe*. More, it also comes to the same conclusion, namely that doing good in a bad world is impossible and so violence is necessary. But that is where the analogy stops. Instead of Chicago, of capitalist speculation and misery or worker revolt, we have a lost hole of a place somewhere in heartland America, community services, and the banality of evil among good people.

So the new Joan of Arc is no longer a parody of Christ, who offers her life up for the people's redemption and discovers the terrestrial realities of class struggle. Grace (who is grace itself) becomes a Christic figure *à la* Dostoyevsky, an envoy from the Elsewhere who encounters the taste of exploitation and humiliation inflicted upon others in the tiniest and most peaceful cells of the social body. The evil incarnated, in particular, by the perversity of the little Jason, who asks Grace for a spanking as a proof of love and then uses it against her, cannot be remedied by any struggle. This is what is shown by the ambiguity of the photographs that accompanies the film's closing credits: photographs by Walker Evans, Dorothea Lange and other photographers, all of whom bear witness to the era of the Great Depression and the social commitment of artists. Simply, we are left wondering whether these photos have been shown to us to remind us of a social injustice which no one can put right, or to have it understood that the famous men of James Agee and Walker Evans have turned into the small monsters of heartland America. But one thing is certain: no longer is it social struggle that measures up to the evil that Grace encounters. The will to do good no longer proves to be a naivety that needs enlightening. The Lord, Grace's father, who reserves all vengeance for himself, is identical to the king of thugs who renders justice to humanity in the form of a radical purging.

This vision of evil and of justice raised some hackles, and not only American ones. The president of the Festival of Cannes explicitly said that a film that is so far removed from human sentiments cannot be awarded a prize. *Mystic River,* no doubt, responds to the criteria of humanism such as they ought to be held by the Cannes Jury. But it also shows us that 'humanism' itself has changed. In former times, humanism was a faith in the human capacity to create a world as just as was permitted by the equally human capacity for weakness. Today, it rather consists in testifying to the impossibility of any such justice. We engage in too much wrongdoing to be able to afford the luxury of being just, such is the meaning of the mute gestures exchanged at the film's end by the unpunished assassin and the cop that shares his secret. Sean and Jimmy are guilty of having once led the timid Dave astray with their street games, guilty of having let get away those paedophiles posing as

policemen, who sequestered and raped him. The trauma suffered was irreparable. And, according to the logic of this irreparability, the adult Dave would be beset with presumptions of guilt in relation to the murder of Jimmy's daughter and become a victim of Jimmy's act of summary justice against him.

The whole structure of the film seems to consist in the distending of a small episode from one of the pioneer films of the American way of the last 30 years: *Once upon a time in America*. The camera of Sergio Leone has us read the decision of a killer in the face of a powerless child whom he will shoot down. It thus has us enter into a confusing collusion with the killer's enjoyment and the child's wait for the inevitable. *Mystic River* similarly presents a long chronicle of a death announced long beforehand. The mental and perceptual landscape of this putting to death – overthrowing the classic scenario of the falsely accused by a scenario of the promised victim – is composed by the nocturnal atmosphere in which David turns – and the camera around him – as if in an aquarium, the gesticulations and howls of Jimmy and his two acolytes and the fury of the organ. The film's moral – the moral that it stages and the moral of its staging – might be summed up thus: since we've all killed a child, it may as well be done properly. Clint Eastwood was complimented for having avoided the various 'manicheisms' of Michael Moore and Lars von Trier. On closer examination, this 'non-manicheism', this acceptance of injustice in the name of evil, we see a homogeneity between it and the prevailing discourse against the axis of Evil. As all of us are savages, all potential murderers, we ought to accept the work of justice. But for the same reason, we must not demand that justice be too just. The struggle against infinite evil will produce blunders, will create victims, in the working class areas of Boston as much as in those of Arab towns.

The film *Elephant* dispenses with all considerations of justice and all causal schemas. If Clint Eastwood's 'Freudianism' resides in its demonstration of irreparable trauma, *Elephant's* lies in its analysis of a psychosis: the adolescents in the film live in an 'innocent' world, a world from which sin, the law and authority are radically absent. The alcoholic, depressed father, whose sons treat him as a child, is the sole representative of the parental instance. But no psychological causality is implied here. John, son of the disgraceful father, is precisely neither culprit nor victim. Throughout the film his presence functions only as that of a witness who assures the continuity throughout the broken narration. And in comparison with the little Jason, its two murderers appear rather candid. No psychology of filiation and its troubles, nor any theology of evil comes to replace the vanished socio-political horizon.

Therein resides the film's entire principle. In contrast to the heaviness of the trauma in which Clint Eastwood's expressionist *mise-en-scene* places us, Gus Van Sant, like Lars von Trier, exhibits a commitment to conceptual abstraction in turning the *mise-en-scene* into the rigorous demonstration of a point of view. This point of view is that there is no reason for crime, other than the very absence of reasons. His *mise-en-scene* is the long manifestation of this absence. The primary school is strangely inhabited. The language laboratory where the killers store their equipment is as deserted as the gymnasium through which the 'uncomfortable-with-himself' adolescent crosses. These rooms present in advance the void that the murderous adolescent will contemplate at the end as his own work. The camera follows at length the twists and turns of bodies filmed from behind through almost deserted corridors. This space without consistency – which is also often fuzzy – already resembles the space of the screen on which the two adolescents order their weapons and on which one of them tests himself on a game of massacre while the other contents himself with massacring Beethoven on the piano. And, in return, it is as some video-game creature on a screen that Alex will appear at the end in the gaze of the two adolescents promised to death. But the end of the film will leave the promised death hanging in suspense.

This suspended end is emblematic of the film's entire method. In the cool room, Alex is framed by sides of meat, enjoying for an eternity from the delay granted to/imposed on the two adolescents; all we hear are their pleading voices. Sergio Leone, naturally, comes again to mind. But these quarters of meat used to frame the child-killer take us even further back in the history of cinema. They bring to mind the abattoirs that Eisenstein introduced symbolically into his film *Strike*, to which so many filmmakers have paid more or less explicit visual homage. But here the symbolic signification (meat/blood/violence) is absorbed. All that remains is the cool room, which condenses the cold of the corridors and empty rooms, like that of the computer screen or the Beethoven 'clair de lune'. Ultimately all that remains is cinema's own self-designation, the commitment of the filmmaker as the constructor of this cool room in which normality and monstrosity, reason and absence of reason enter into equivalence. The final shot tells us: all this is only a film.

The staging of the killers and that of the filmmaker, then, are mirrored in one another. The filmmaker, like the killers, puts into play a principle of interruption. In his cool room just like in the room and on the screen of the two killers, the endless wandering through the corridors and the interminable circulation of empty words – those of the three small parakeets or of the association homo-hetero – become blocked, framed, subject to a principle of closure. The film's lesson would lie here. It posits a good kind of interruption to respond to the bad kind. 'Make love, not war', people used to say in the times of violence. 'Make films, not massacres', such would be, with Gus Van Sant, the formula of an ethics suited to those of evil. Unfortunately not everybody can make cinema.

CHAPTER TWENTY-NINE
Criminal Democracy? *March 2004*

A few months ago in France, there appeared a work intriguingly titled: *Les Penchants criminels de l'Europe démocratique.*[1] The author, Jean-Claude Milner, did not leave readers in the dark for long as to the crime of which democracy was, according to him, guilty. Via the extreme subtleness of a demonstration that mobilizes all the resources of philosophy and linguistics, of psychoanalysis and of history, the argument advanced is simple. The crime that European democracy bears within it, quite simply, is the extermination of the Jews of Europe. There would be little point in responding that the Nazi regime that had planned this extermination was not clamouring for democracy. The argument, precisely, is inverted: what, according to Milner, made the construction of a Europe resting on the principle of democracy possible after 1945 is precisely the fact that Nazism, in the years preceding, had eliminated the element that thwarted its advent, namely the existence of a strong Jewish community in Europe.

This unverifiable historical argument clearly needed backing up by a theoretical argument, which runs as follows: the reign of modern democracy is one of a society that will consider no limit to its powers. This limitlessness is illustrated in particular in contemporary dreams of genetic manipulation, which abolish the last difference between nature and artifice and give children created *in vitro* to homosexual couples. Now, the tendency of modern democratic society to want to take its limitless power to the point of abolishing filiation encounters an irreducible enemy: the people who gather under the principle of filiation and transmission, that is, the Jewish people. The conclusion followed as a matter of course: in annihilating the Jews, Hitler realized the intimate dream of democracy and allowed it to prevail in Europe.

As extreme as it is, this demonstration has no trouble blending into the present-day landscape of political and philosophical thought. This landscape, we know, endured a major change during the 1980s. Until then, the so-called western world laid claim to a certain idea of democracy, conceived as a juridico-political system. Accordingly some contrast its universal law and individual liberties to totalitarian coercion. Others denounced the reality of economic exploitation and class domination concealed beneath its universal forms. Real democracy against formal democracy or, conversely, the rights of democratic man against totalitarianism – such was the landscape. The opposition, doubtless, authorized a few mediations: the partisans of real democracy could show themselves to be more attentive in the defence of formal liberties than the champions of liberal democracy themselves. And the latter, from their side, would blame democracy's weaknesses or excesses for the advent of totalitarian regimes. But it was too far to leap from there to the idea that the extermination of the Jews was the direct realization of the democratic principle.

To overcome such a baffling logical leap, the landscape of political thought had to undergo a serious upheaval. This upheaval has indeed occurred, but it also took a form at first sight paradoxical. On the one hand, since the beginning of the 1980s, the denunciation of totalitarianism has become more radical and more insistent than ever before. But on the other, the distinction between the totalitarianism denounced and democracy has tended to become increasingly tenuous.

On the one hand, the end of the Soviet system has been accompanied by a meticulous inventory that turns the whole history of communism into a long list of crimes, minutely detailed in thick 'black books'. At the same time, an entirely new sort of attention has been brought to bear on the Nazi genocide. This found expression not only with the multiplication of testimonies but also in a current of thought for which the death camps became a radical event in whose light the whole history of the last two centuries had to be reconceived.

Here is where the paradox appears. We might have thought that the collapse of the Soviet alternative and the new ledger of Nazi and Soviet crimes might reinforce the fragile western faith in the virtues of democracy. Nothing of the sort transpired, quite to the contrary. The more that these regimes' crimes came under a new sort of public light, the more the former champions of western and democratic human rights turned against their idol of yesterday. The fiercest condemners of Soviet crimes were, like the historian Francois Furet, the first to see it as the direct consequence of the French Revolution. One would still have been able, it is true, to condemn the excesses of the revolutionary 'government of the people' and oppose to them the human rights proclaimed by the American liberal revolution. But these rights too quickly came under suspicion. These were times in which American sociologists, in the wake of Daniel Bell, began to condemn the damaging effects of mass individualism for ruining of all forms of public authority. Taking up the baton, French political scientists, such as Marcel Gauchet, then construed human rights as the precise expression of this mass democratic individualism, harmful not only to authority but to the very sense of political community.

So, step-by-step, the traditional oppositions tended to vanish. The revolutionary crowds and their unrest came to be identified with the dispersion caused by the egotistical and narcissistic individuals of democratic society. And the democratic effect of 'undoing bonds' were identified with totalitarian catastrophe. This made it possible, with Giorgio Agamben, to show that the Rights of Man involved a confusion between the citizen-identity and bare life and to find its logic being carried out both in the Nazi genocide and in the everyday life our democracies. One could, then, with Jean-Claude Milner, see democracy as the very principle of genocide.

The remaining problem was to find the good form of government that counters this democracy no longer distinguishable from totalitarianism. Some have called it a republic and so emphasized the virtue of the good republican government against the anarchy of democratic individuals regulated by their simple good pleasure. Jean-Claude Milner, for his part, chose a blunter term. He has called it pastoral government.

This doing, he recalls the very old origins of current discourses on democracy. It was Plato, in the *Republic,* who painted the picture of the democratic city so endlessly reprised by our sociologists: democracy, he said, is that charming regime in which all are free and do exactly as they please: not only men but also women and children and even horses and asses, whose democratic pride pushes them to occupy the street and knock passers-by over. This is the indocile democratic ass that we still find being discussed in the self-satisfied descriptions of the society of good, unlimited pleasure in which workers who always want more and the jobless, drunk with new forms of enjoyment, ruin the republican community with their senseless demands. But the condemnation of the indocile ass, doubtless, conceals a more profound trouble. In democracy, Plato tells us, governors appear as the governed, and the governed the governors. We understand, then, that the true scandal of democracy does not reside in the unrest of the masses or the licence of individuals. It resides simply in the fact that in it governing comes to appear as an activity that is purely contingent, not founded on any title that is granted by birth, age, knowledge or a supposedly manifest superiority. Democracy is the form of government that is based on the idea that no individual or any group has a title to govern over others.

This contingent government of anyone at all testifies, for Plato, to a world which runs upside down. There was a time when the world guided by divinity ran as it should: a time when authority took on the air of the enlightened solicitude of the pastor who knows what is best for his flock. It is this pastoral government – in which the elites exhibit paternal concern for their flock and protect it from its own rebellious spirits – that, in the West, is increasingly loudly dreamt of today. But the matter of who is to educate these pastors and by what signs we can recognize their wisdom remains rather obscure.

CHAPTER THIRTY
The Difficult Legacy of Michel Foucault,
June 2004

In this very month, Michel Foucault will have been dead for 20 years. A new occasion has thus arisen for a commemoration, popular as they are in France. This anniversary, however, is more problematic than that of Sartre's 4 years ago. For this latter occasion, it was necessary to produce a major operation of reconciliation in order to extricate the provocative philosopher from the 'extremist' causes in which he had compromised himself, so that he could be introduced into the national pantheon of writers and thinkers, the friends of liberty. The case of Foucault is more complex. The philosopher and activist has no excesses that must be pardoned in the name of his virtues. For, precisely, one does not know what the activist should be reproached for, nor with what the philosopher should be credited. More radically, there is a serious uncertainty in understanding the relation between the one and the other.

This uncertainty receives expression in the debates over Foucault's legacy. One of them concerns his relation to the cause of sexual minorities. In *La Volonté de savoir*,[1] in fact, Foucault put forward a provocative argument: the notion of 'sexual repression' actually works to mask the inverse operation, the efforts of power to get us to speak about sex, to oblige individuals to over-invest in the secrets and the promises that it detained. Some were keen, notably in the United States, to infer from this an invalidation of the forms of identity politics to which sexual minorities were committed. Conversely, with David Halperin's *Saint Foucault*,[2] the philosopher was enthroned as the patron saint of the *queer*

movement for his denouncing of the game of sexual identities that the homophobic tradition had set up. In France the polemic developed on another terrain. Indeed, one of the editors of Foucault's *Dits et Écrits*,[3] Francois Ewald, is today the appointed theoretician of a bosses union, and is committed, in the name of the morality of risk, to continuing the struggle against the French system of social protection. Hence, the question that worked the polemicists: can a programme of struggle against social security be drawn from the Foucauldian critique of the 'society of control'?

Some have aimed to rise above these debates and attempted to draw out the philosophical foundations of Foucault's politics. These are generally sought for in the analysis of biopower that he once sketched. Others, with Michael Hardt and Toni Negri, have equipped him with the substratum of a philosopher of life, which he himself never took the time to elaborate, in a bid to assimilate biopolitics to the movement of the multitudes breaking open the shackles of Empire. Others still, like Giorgio Agamben, have assimilated Foucault's description of 'the power over life' to a generalized regime of the state of exception, common to democracies and totalitarian regimes alike. And still others see Foucault as a theoretician of ethics and enjoin us to discover – between his scholarly studies on asceticism in antiquity and his small confidences in the contemporary pleasures of the sauna – the principles of a new morality of the subject.

All these enterprises have one point in common. They hope to ascertain in Foucault's trajectory a principle of finality that would assure the coherence of the whole and provide a solid basis for a new politics or a novel ethics. They want to see in him a confirmation of the idea of the philosopher who synthesizes knowledge and teaches us the rules of action.

Now, this idea of the philosopher and of the concordance between knowledge, thought and life is precisely the one that Foucault challenged, through his approach even more than his statements. What he foremost invented was an original way of doing philosophy. When phenomenology was promising us – at the end of its abstractions – access to the 'things themselves' and to the 'world of life', and when some were dreaming of making this promised world coincide with the one that Marxism promised the workers, he practiced a maximum distance. He did not promise life. He was fully in it, in the decisions of the police, the cries of the imprisoned or the examination of the bodies of the ill. But he did not say to us what we could do with this 'life' and with its knowledge. Much rather, he saw it as the refutation in act of discourses of consciousness [*conscience*] and of the human that back then underpinned the hopes of liberated tomorrows. More than any other 'structuralist' theoretician, Foucault was accused of being a thinker of technocratism, of turning our society and our thought into a machine defined by ineluctable and anonymous functionings.

We know how the 68 years would overturn things. Between the creation of the *Université de Vincennes* and the founding of the Group of Information on Prisons, the structuralist 'technocrat' figured among the top rung of intellectuals in which the anti-authoritarian movement recognized itself. Everything suddenly became obvious: he who had analysed the birth of medical power and the great confinement of the mad and the marginal was perfectly predisposed to symbolize a movement which attacked not only the relations of production and the visible institutions of the state, but all the forms of power that are disseminated throughout the social body. One photograph would sum up this logic: in it we see Foucault, armed with a microphone, alongside his old enemy Sartre, rousing some demonstrators who had gathered together to condemn a racist crime. The photo is titled 'the philosophers are in the street'.

But a philosopher's being in the street does not suffice for his philosophy to ground the movement, nor even his own presence there. The philosophical displacement operated by Foucault implied precisely upsetting the relations between positive knowledge, philosophical consciousness and action. In abandoning itself to the examination of the real functioning by which effective thought acts on bodies, philosophy abdicates its central position. But the knowledge that it yields does not thus form any weapon of the masses in the Marxist manner. It simply constitutes a new map on the terrain of this effective and decentered thought. It does not provide the revolt with a consciousness. But it permits the network of its reasons to find the network of reasons of those who, here or there, exploit their knowledge and their own reason to introduce the grain of sand that jams the machine.

The archaeology of the relations of power and of the workings of thought, then, founds revolt no more than it does subjugation. It redistributes the maps and the territories. In subtracting thought from its royal place, it gives right to that of each and all of us, that notably of the 'infamous men' whose lives Foucault had undertaken to write. By the same token, however, it prohibits thought, restored to all, from taking any central position in the encounter between knowledge and power. This does not mean that politics loses itself in the multiplicity of power relations everywhere disseminated. It means, first of all, that it is always a leap that no knowledge justifies and which no knowledge administers. The passage from knowledge to an intervention supposes a singular relay, the sentiment of something intolerable.

'The situation in the prisons is intolerable', Foucault declared in 1971 with the founding of the Groups of Information on Prisons. This 'intolerable' did not come from some self-evidence piece of knowledge and was not addressed to some universal consciousness that would be compelled to accept it. It was only a 'sentiment', the same one, no doubt, that had pushed the philosopher to commit himself to the unknown terrain of archives without knowing where it would lead him, and still less where it might lead others. Some months later, however, the intolerable sentiment of the philosopher would be forced to encounter that which the prisoners in revolt in several French prisons declared with their own weapons based upon their own knowledge. Thought does not transmit itself to action. Instead thought transmits itself to a thought and action which provokes another. Thought acts insofar as it accepts not to know very well what is pushing it and renounces to assert control over its effects.

The paradox is that Foucault himself seems to have found it difficult to accept this entirely. We know that he stopped writing for a long while. It occurred right after *La Volonté de savoir,* the book around which today's exegetes vie. This book aimed in principle to be an introduction to a *Histoire de la sexualité,* whose signification it summed up in advance. It seems that Foucault came to fear the path that he had mapped out in advance. Before the imminence of death pushed him to publish *L'Usage des plaisirs* and *Le Souci de soi,* he had not published anything save interviews.[4] In these interviews, of course, he was asked to say what it was that linked his patient investigations in the archives with his interventions on the repression in Poland, his delving into the Greek techniques of subjectivation and his work with a union confederation. All his responses, as we clearly sense, comprise so many deceptions that reintroduce a place of mastery which his very own work had undermined.

The same holds for all those rationalizations that purport to draw from his writings either the principle of the queer revolution, that of the emancipation of the multitudes or that of a new ethics of the individual. There is not a body of Foucauldian thought that founds a new politics or a new ethics. There are books which produce effects to the very extent that they do not say to us what we must do with them. The embalmers are going to have a tough time of it.

CHAPTER THIRTY-ONE
The New Reasons for the Lie, *August 2004*

At the summer's start a news item shook France. A young woman travelling in a suburban train with her baby was robbed and battered by a gang of black and Maghrebin adolescents. Seeing, as they stole her papers, that she was born in the 'posh suburbs', they concluded that she was Jewish. Consequently, the robbery turned into an anti-Semitic attack: they scarred her face with a knife, painted swastikas over her and cut her hair savagely. None of the train's passengers had intervened to defend the young woman and her baby, not even, simply, to pull the alarm signal.

Within 48 hours, we saw declarations from politicians and commentaries in newspapers proliferate. Even more than the attack, it was the passiveness of the commuters that provoked indignation. The monstrous behaviour of these youths appeared as a reality that was unfortunately all too explainable: newspaper columnists did not cease to evoke the wrongdoings of small gangs of youths from the poor suburbs, often with an immigrant background. The reality of tensions between the Jewish and Muslim communities is also very present as are the attacks against Jewish persons and institutions that have occurred over recent months. But how are we to explain the complicit passiveness of the commuters? *Le Monde* thus ran two sorts of commentary side-by-side. A sociologist explained that the young Maghrebi of the poor suburbs were sending back to society the image that the latter made of them: that of brutal, macho and fanatical youths. An editorialist made clear that the commuters' behaviour testified to something of a far more serious nature: a phenomenon of collective cowardice, of the collapse of the most traditional collective values. The event thereby reflected back to society the image of a twofold decomposition: on the one hand, small gangs of savages; on the other, an apathetic mass of egotistical individuals.

Two days later, we learnt that the whole affair was a pure and simple fabrication. The young woman had done it to attract the attention of a companion who had not been sensitive enough to her problems.

False news is as old as the world, as is using it in the framework of inter-community conflicts. This false news, however, seems to testify to a new regime of lying. Two traditional forms of mass lie are more than familiar to us. There is the form of the 'popular rumour' whereby in the Middle Ages, for example, Jews were accused of kidnapping children for ritual murders. And there is the form of lie that is deliberately made up by an authority, state or other, as an expedient way of stirring up hatred against a community that serves as a scapegoat.

The lie told by the young Marie Léonie does not fit into either of these two frames. The information machine of our times goes quicker than any popular rumour. Moreover, our consensual governments have no interest in fuelling wars between communities. So, it is not possible in this case to blame either the 'gullibility' of the popular masses or the perverse imagination of men of power. But this lie is not, for all that, a purely individual creation. By the very way in which it simulates a 'societal phenomenon' for private ends, it testifies to a new form of the false. This form is not linked to any excess or lack but to the normal functioning of the information machine, to the normal relation between information and power in our societies. The 'individual' invention of this racist attack was possible and plausible because the social machine of fabrication and of the interpretation of events in a certain sense expected the event.

Let's be more specific. At stake here is not to say, with certain critics of the media, that the televisual screen has rendered reality and simulacrum equivalent, and that the events no longer have any need of really existing because their images exist without them. Regardless of what the critics say, the image does not constitute the heart of media power and of its utilization by the authorities. The heart of the information machine is interpretation. No events, not even false ones, are needed because their interpretations are already there, because they pre-exist them and call them forth. From this viewpoint, the unanimous indignation against the 'cowardice' of the witnesses is significant.

From the fact that no witness manifested himself, none of the commentators drew the simplest conclusion, if not a single witness to the event did anything, perhaps this is because the event did not take place. What is intolerable in the eyes of the moralistic journalist is the very idea that nothing has happened. It is the lack of events. The interpretation must, then, be turned upside down: if there was no witness, it is because the witnesses made a show of their cowardice. And is it this cowardice which becomes the heart of the event itself, the societal phenomenon to be delved into.

For the machine to turn, there must always be events. This does not simply mean that in order to sell papers there has to be a bit of sensationalism. At stake is not simply to scribble on paper. Material must be furnished for the interpretative machine. This machine does not always need something to happen. It needs a certain type of thing to happen, things called 'societal phenomena': that is, particular events that happen to ordinary people at some point within society, but also events that constitute symptoms – events which invite an interpretation but an interpretation that is already there in front of them. For, ultimately, the interpretation given always amounts to the same explanation in two points: first, that modern society is troubled because it is not modern enough, because there are groups which are not yet really modern, which still carry the same traditional tribal values; and second, modern society is troubled because it is too modern, because it too quickly lost the sense of the collective solidarities which characterized traditional societies and that in it everyone is indifferent to everyone else. The barbarism of yet-to-be-socialized youths inhabiting the poor suburbs, and the indifference of the ordinary passengers of public transport. The extraordinary nature of the imaginary attack suffered by Marie Léonie is a mere repeat of the ordinariness of the interpreting machine.

This is not just a simple matter of the constraint weighing on a media prey to the hard law of sales and audience ratings. It is a matter of the mode of exercise and of legitimation of the social and state machine. This is what explains the celerity, indeed the imprudence, with which the French leaders reacted. It is true that they have no interest in spreading news liable to stir up quarrels between communities. But they do have a vital interest in showing their vigilance with regard to everything which can generate such quarrels, their attentive ear to all 'societal phenomena' that expresses some discontentment in the social body.

Our governments have no need of lies to excite crowds. But they do need events and interpretations because it is their legitimacy itself that is constituted by this continuous collection of facts and incessant reading of symptoms. The consensual order represents itself as that of the great family in which the leaders are foremost doctors who attend to all the symptoms of an incubating sickness, indeed even of an ill-being liable to engender fantasies that jeopardize the collective health. The risk of sanctioning a false symptom is, then, less than that of missing a true one, and above all to that of not appearing to be interested in them. The paternal concern of governments is thereby in harmony with the activity of a society tirelessly taken up with the task of its self-examination and self-interpretation. The essential thing is that there are always events to interpret, symptoms to decipher. A famous theatre joke has it that a man in good health is a sick person who does not yet know it. Today this logic has become the global logic of a society where a non-event is always an event that has not yet cottoned onto the fact that it is one.

CHAPTER THIRTY–TWO
Beyond Art? *October 2004*

The visitor entering the door of the Biennale de Sao Paulo is immedi-ately enthralled: facing him is a 'Cauchemar de George V' showing a tiger attacking an elephant; to his right extends a scenery of pyramids, similar to the scale models of archaeology museums; to his left, there are sewing machines on which women are weaving threads, as if they are working on the scenery surrounding them – squares in patchworks on which urban or rustic decors are arranged on foam rubber covered with coloured fabrics, evoking both stuffed toys for children and con-struction games, to mark an interrogation into the economic trans-formations and identity mutations occurring in contemporary China.

Continuing further, the visitor will encounter, notably, a fishing boat from the Nordeste that evokes the crossing from Portugal to Brazil, a dream house made of fabrics, a Mongolian tent, a 'Puzzle Polis II', which arranges, in the form of a town, lamps that have the shape of highrises or of the cars of a shantytown artist; one hundred and ninety eight por-traits of Chinese peasants, placed side by side like a great fresco; an assemblage of many tens of photographs representing a Mali living room for all social conditions, ethnicities or religions; photographs of a small Polish town testifying to post-socialist misery; photographs of sordid scenes from heartland America testifying to the underneath of capitalist prosperity; some small photographs of ordinary Ukrainians stuck onto grand kitsch decors of parks abounding with ponds and swans.

It is commonplace for nostalgics to claim that contemporary art is the reign of 'anything goes'. The judgement is too global to teach us any-thing. The putative 'anything goes' is always a something, a determin-ate mixture, testifying to a given state of relations between forms of art and objects, images or uses of ordinary life. At the Biennale of Sao Paolo, as at so many contemporary exhibitions, it is not the fantasy of artists beholden to their caprice that reigns. The visitor is rather struck by the similarities between the artists' preoccupations and chosen procedures, regardless of whether they are Chinese or American, Brazilian, Indonesian or Slovak. No doubt the organizer's choice of theme – the city – also created part of the unity. But the thematic choice itself reflects a very broad tendency: a sort of obsession with, indeed a fanaticism of, the real.

This obsession with the real takes many forms. It can reside in a concern to bear witness to the state of the world through the objectivity of the photographic apparatus, rendering exactly the scenery of ordinary life at the hour of globalization. It can involve the desire to mix the images of everyday culture or the object of popular art with the conceptual arrangements of artists. Taking place simultaneously in Rio de Janeiro, an exhibition called *Tudo e Brasil* testified to the recurrent dream of a Brazilian art able to unify constructivist modernism with forms of popular art or culture: great abstract paintings comprising a multiplicity of dominos or pieces of a football, or video works inventorying the art of tagging and of street painting. This obsession can also reside in the will to create real objects, objects freed from the irreality of the painted canvas or the mediations of photographic reproduction and able promptly to impose their reality in the three dimensions of space: a house, a tent, a boat . . . It is as if the refusal of the simulacrum of representation was proceeding in the opposite direction to that which stamped art in the time of Malevitch or Mondrian: no longer the abstract painting but instead really existing objects as things of the world. In the *Cratylus,* Plato evoked the limit towards which resemblance tends, at the risk of abolishing itself in it. This limit is the object which is absolutely similar to the model, the double which no longer distinguishes itself from the real thing. The abiding name for this attempt to make of the sign or of the image not longer an indice or a copy of the thing, but the thing itself, is cratylism. And haunting this biennale was indeed a cratylism not unlike that to be found in so many other manifestations of contemporary art.

But the obsession with the real can also emphasize the act which intervenes directly in social reality. The walls of contemporary exhibitions often include photographs or videos that take stock of such interventions: provocations such as Gianni Motti's placing himself, in his staging of a political fiction, at the core of state secrets, or Santiago Sierra's paying Moroccan sub-proletarians to mime their exploitation by digging their own graves. Provocation, however, is not what is at issue in a work shown at the Biennale by Cuban artist, René Francisco. With a group of artists, he devoted the money he received from an artistic foundation to conducting a survey of the needs of inhabitants from a poor suburb. It does not suffice, however, to conduct a survey of needs. The needs must also be met. The video René Francisco thus shows us artists/artisans busy fixing the plumbing and painting the house of an old couple whose shadows on the canvass are watching them.

'Is this art?' the aesthetes will ask. The question is badly formed. The fact is that modern art as a whole has been moved by the concern to leave itself in order to transform the actual reality of things. The pioneers of abstract painting, reduced to its essence as an arrangement of coloured forms, also championed a kind of art that would be art no longer, that would transform itself into a form of common life. To make 'painting' no longer, not as separate reality, but to construct the forms of life and the furniture of a new life – such was the dream common to both Mondrian and Malevitch. And it provided the ground for the artistic avant-garde's adhesion to the creation of the Soviet 'new life'.

What is new and significant is therefore not the will of an art acting directly on the world. It is the form that this will take today: individual assistance to the most destitute there were once rejected both by the artistic avant-garde and the constructors of socialism. The dream of an art that builds forms for a new life has become the modest project of 'relational art': a kind of art that no longer strives to create works but instead situations of relations, and in which the artist, as a French theoretician of this art says, renders to society 'little services' designed to repair 'the cracks in the social bond'.[1] The irony is obviously that at the Biennale the representatives of this aesthetics of art *qua* social service were artists from the last remaining countries that subscribe to Marxist socialism.

There would be little interest in accusing the naivety of artists or the cunning of the exhibition organizers. Because this obsession with the real, this feverish will to 'make or do' something whether a solid object, an effective act or a testimony on the state of the world, also reflects the singular stance of artistic activity in a universe in which not only do the great revolutionary projects tend to disappear but so also the forms of political conflict themselves. The void of the political scene incites the artists and the actors of the art world to put the means and sites at their disposal to testify to a reality of inequalities, of contradictions and of conflicts which consensual discourse tends to render invisible and to suggest ways of intervening against the reigning fatalism. The problem is that the undeniable efforts of many artists to break with the dominant consensus and undermine the existing order tends to enlist in the framework of consensual description and categories, returning the artistic powers of provocation to the ethical tasks of witnessing a world in common and of providing assistance to the most disempowered.

CHAPTER THIRTY-THREE
The Politics of Images, *February 2005*

Two contemporary historical and cinematic topics have once again raised a recurrent question. The first is the sixtieth anniversary of the entry of the allied troops in Auschwitz, the second the release of the film *The Downfall* which recounts the last days of Adolf Hitler in his bunker. And the question: what must or must not be shown of the great Nazi enterprise and of its outcome – the extermination of the Jews of Europe?

The question obviously contains two questions. The first is about historical fiction in general and asks: how are we to reconcile the requisites of fiction and those of history? Before the age of modern revolutions, this question was barely raised: historians recounted the high deeds of princes and generals; grand poetry narrated the thoughts, sentiments and actions of characters situated above commoners. For two centuries, however, the maps of the fictional and of the historic have been redistributed, as have those of the great and the small. Fiction has decreed the equality of all before its law; history has found itself torn between the decisions of state and the slow and obscure life of the multitudes. Historical fiction has become the interweaving of these two logics. It shows us the great deeds of history through the perspective of the small people and the upheavals of private lives. In this vein, *The Downfall* based itself on a book written by a historian about Hitler's last days and the testimonies of it by one of the *Führer's* former secretaries. Wim Wenders strongly reproached the filmmaker for this mixture on the grounds that it enables the author to dispense with having a point of view. But the same reproach could be made to Hugo or to Tolstoy: *Les Misérables* and *War and Peace* are formed around this exact oscillation. It was Tolstoy who elaborated its theory and the formula has subsequently been reprised by countless novelists and filmmakers.

So, the reproach has hardly any significance in itself. In fact, it obscures an entirely different problem. By becoming part of the verisimilitudes of fiction and the familiarity of embodied characters, the deeds of famous men are brought closer to us, are related to the bodies to which we are sensitive, to systems of explanation that justify them. Fiction must be accepted; but how can it be without rendering acceptable that which it shows, on this occurrence the murderous madness of a system? To insist that the author take up a viewpoint means requiring him to contradict this natural logic of fiction, to introduce the unacceptable into the acceptable.

What forms must this unacceptable take? In *The Downfall* we never stop hearing the monstrous remarks of Hitler or his adepts, or seeing unbearable spectacles: amputated bodies, brains blown out by revolvers, the glacial ceremonial of Mrs Goebbels poisoning her six children one after the other. But the monstrous ramblings are those of a used man, a man confined to his bunker and his delirium, akin to one of those mad kings we see at the theatre. Mrs Goebbels' monstrous meticulousness revives memories of ancient heroes protecting themselves and their family from servitude. All the blood-drenched bodies belong to a vanquished people, and there is always some commiseration for the defeated. If the everyday ordinariness of the bunker works to trivialize the Nazi crime, the extraordinariness of the words and of the monstrous acts tips it over into tragic terror.

Some will say that the trial is a trap from the start: what is represented is the defeat of Nazism. Only, what must be judged is not its defeat but its prior 'victories', the monstrous order that it set up. What the film is missing are its veritable victims: not generals who have their brains blown out but first of all the six million dead of the extermination camps.

Unfortunately, the same problem arises from this side. And the choice of the films presented by the television stations to commemorate Auschwitz restaged the same question: how are the camps to be shown? Obviously not by means of actual images: they are missing due to the very logic of the process which effaced its own traces. Or, then, by means of a fiction of the type used in *Holocaust,* that is by recounting the fate of some of the individuals caught in the process, from the side of the henchmen or that of the victims? But our empathy with the tragic destiny of the Weiss family is immediately dubious. Does sharing in the misfortunes of a suffering family not imply forgetting what this family is supposed to incarnate: the fate of an entire people? Does not commiseration that we feel for those about to enter the gas chamber and even our identification with the combatants of the ghetto produce a counter-effect? They render present those whose existence, and even traces, the Nazi plan aimed to eliminate. Our commiseration therefore prevents us from any level-headed consideration of the monstrosity of the overall plan to exterminate a collective and the silence with which this process was accomplished.

The second problem might thus be formulated as follows: how are we to give a fictional form to the exceptional crime of the extermination? It has become commonplace to compare the *Holocaust's* sentimental trivialization with the rigour of *Shoah*. Claude Lanzmann's film, in fact, simultaneously refuses all historical images and any fictionalization of history. He strives to render the past present only in the speech of the survivors before the silence of the sites of extermination. He thereby claims to have avoided two forms of trivialization: that of the fiction which effaces the extermination by rendering bodies present; and that of the historical document which finds reasons that place it within a more extensive chain of causes and effects.

The good representation of the extermination therefore would be one that separates out the horror of the crime from every image that brings it closer to our sensibility, from every explanation that provides it with a reason makes it acceptable to our intelligence. It would be the representation of the unrepresentable. But the following question immediately arises: what does the goodness of this representation consist in? An oft-repeated saying provides a prompt response: those who ignore their past are doomed to relive it. It is therefore necessary, we are told, to observe a 'duty of memory' and to examine the past closely to prevent its recurrence. But what are we to understand by this exactly? The expression can mean two things: first, that the horror must be shown in its sensory reality so as to induce the feeling of the intolerable that brings us to repel the ideas that spawned the horror; or else that we must show how these ideas themselves were spawned so that our knowledge of the process in turn spawns the means to prevent its reproduction. Only, the purism of the good representation renders both these deductions null and void. To put bodies suffering the intolerable into images also means offering them up to sentimental commiseration or perverse voyeurism. To present the reasons for the extermination is to present it with a justification. The horror of the extermination must remain without any cause other than the monstrosity of its proper project. But then no effect is to be expected from knowledge of the past. The politics of memory is self-contradictory. And the good representation is no more certain of its effect than the bad one.

Here we come to the bottom of the matter. The opposition between good and bad ways of representing history confounds two problems. On the one hand, it defines norms of acceptability. So it protests against representations that transform criminals into men like others. It supposes that we are less sensitive to Hitlerian barbarism if we see the dictator moved by his dog or displaying affection towards his secretary. But it also strives to turn these norms of acceptability into principles of utility. Now, why would an image of Hitler patting his dog or his secretary be more useful to the cause of combating Nazism? Why would the representation of the extermination as a disembodied mechanics be more appropriate to feeding hatred of anti-Semitism than that of the suffering of the victims or the inner states of the executioners? We can always find some criteria to say that *Shoah* is a more appropriate way than *Holocaust* to transmit the monstrosity of the genocide and to respect the memory of its victims. Deducing from this their respective abilities to prohibit equivalent forms of monstrosity in future is an altogether different thing. Between the good way of speaking about the past horror and the useful way of preventing the horror in the future there is no necessary link. This pious way of thinking, which aims to use its knowledge of the past to guarantee the future, still clings perhaps to the times of princes and of their advisers who would teach them the examples to follow in order to govern peoples and win battles.

CHAPTER THIRTY-FOUR
Democracy and Its Doctors, *May 2005*

Unrest hit the French and European governmental staff after several polls showed that the French might vote 'no' in the referendum to ratify the European Constitution. How is such a thing possible, it was asked, when both the conservative government and the socialist opposition called to vote 'yes'? This is because, came the response, the French have not understood. They want to express their discontentment with their government, in forgetting that they are not being asked for their opinion about this government but about a treaty that binds 25 European states. But if they do not understand the question being asked, this is no doubt due to the effect of a discontentment, the discontentment of a nation melancholically contemplating its irreversible decline.

Do the French feel worse today than they did 10 or 20 years ago? The question is difficult to answer. And it is perhaps not necessary. For the diagnostic, in any case, precedes the disorder. There are no surprising or disappointing electoral results that do not immediately give rise to this ready explanation: people did not vote as they should have because they did not understand the choice they had been presented. They did not understand this choice because they are suffering a disorder. And the discontentment that they feel is because they belong to economic groups, social classes or national states that are in decline.

So, more than the supposed disorder of the ill, what merits our attention is what is expressed by the reasoning of its doctors – this medicalization of opinion, this interpretation of every vote that does not conform to the official expectations as an expression of a pathological state. If an electoral body is asked the question of whether it is for or against a measure proposed by its government, then the proposition must actually include the possibility of a negative response. This is what, they say, distinguishes our democratic countries from those in which governments are unperturbedly elected by a little less, or even a little more than 100 per cent of the electors. So why is there so much surprise and desolation when the free, unpredictable choice included in the rights granted to citizens is actually translated in act or threatens to be as an unforeseen response? What is the meaning of this strange structure whereby the free choice accorded to popular suffrage actually turns out to be a test of its ability to discern the correct response and of the state of health which enables it to do so or prevents it from doing so?

Heaping doubt on the validity of popular decision did not begin yesterday. What is new today is that it is decried by those who exult its principle. For a long while, such condemnation was left to the 'elites', who bemoaned the fact that the choice of government was left to the mercy of the 'rabble'. Then, the Marxists came along, denouncing the illusion of formal democracy concealing behind it a reality of class struggle and domination. Today, it is the governments of so-called democratic regimes who find this principle disquieting. They claim to be representative of the free choice of their fellow citizens. But they immediately bemoan the fact that their proposed measures are also at the mercy of this free choice.

For these measures, according to them, are not the preserves of free choice but of the necessity of things. If the electoral test doubles up as a test of intelligence and of the health of the electoral body, this is because we live under the regime of a twofold legitimacy. Our governments base their authority on two opposed systems of reasons: on the one hand, it is based on the virtue of popular decision; on the other, on the ability that is theirs, and which the people who chose them are in principle missing: an ability to choose the good solutions that will solve societal problems. Only, these good solutions can be recognized by the fact that they didn't have to be chosen but rather follow from a knowledge of the objective state of things, which is a matter for expert knowledge, not for free choice. The virtue of governments, which distinguishes them from the people that choose them, is that they know how to distinguish between what can be chosen – that is, themselves – and what cannot be: the state of things and the solutions that they propose to bring to it.

There was a time when harmony between the expert knowledge that legitimates the action of governments and the free popular choice that legitimates their existence was presupposed. Today these two principles tend to dissociate themselves, albeit without being able to divorce. And it is to fill up this gap that the electoral process adopts this strange aspect of being a pedagogical test and a therapeutic process. On the one hand, this process increasingly resembles the exercises of school maieutics, in which the schoolmaster who knows the right response pretends not to know it and to be leaving it to the initiative of the students to find it out. But in pedagogical rationale the master wins every time: he demonstrates either the excellence of the students educated by his method or their inability to find the right response without him. For our governors the exercise is more perilous. It is the inability of their students which establishes their competence but this inability first risks working against them.

So the pedagogical exercise is transformed into the crude psychoanalysis of the sick social body. Hence the importance of these exercises of simulation called polls and of the enormous work of interpretation that governments, experts and journalists expend in their regard to show to the sovereign people that it is merely a sick population if it believes it can really choose, and consequently adopt, the suicidal position involved in refusing reality. The electoral process is then transformed into a psychoanalytic cure in which the population is enjoined to fear itself at it moves closer to the edge of the abyss of negation and by this means to regain its mental equilibrium.

The European referendum has brought this logic out into broad daylight. Those who want to conjure away the risks of a negative popular suffrage essentially employ two arguments. First, that this European Constitution does not change anything that was not already there. All the clauses that provoke the cries of its opponents, decrying Europe's 'liberal' drift, were already effective in the extant framework. So it is vain to protest against it today. Second, that there is no 'alternative solution'. Those with twisted minds might respond that the two arguments contradict one another: if everything is similar to what was before, there is no need for an alternative solution and perhaps no need of a new Constitution. But to respond in this way they would denounce themselves as twisted, as *negative souls*. For the argument is simply that they must say *yes* to what is, since if they do not say yes to what is, they say yes to its contrary, namely nothingness. The argument is that they must be affirmative and not negative.

This, in fact, is the only way to make both principles of legitimacy coincide: the expert knowledge which identifies that which is and sets the means to adapt to it, and the popular vote which is proclaimed sovereign over the choice of its governors but is unable to be over the determination of the reality which forms the subject of their government. Herein resides the stakes of a constitution of supranational spaces like Europe: a blurring of the relation between the sovereign people and the space of sovereignty. Things would be simple if at issue was only to replace the small national states with a larger one that would encompass them. But this is not what is at stake. The European Constitution is not, in fact, a Constitution. It is not the emanation of any people and does not found any state. But this Constitution which is not one draws, by the same token, a new map of the relations between a sovereign people and a competent state. It distends the relation between the symbolic space in which sovereignty of the first and the material space in which state and interstate competence is exercised. It completes the effort of our states to institute the space of a coexistence free of confusion between the legitimacy of popular suffrage and that of expert knowledge.

Here is in fact the bottom of the problem. It does not concern the ill-being of such-and-such a people or such-and-such a group. It concerns the relation between parliamentary states with the popular suffrage that legitimates them, the relations of 'democracies' with their own name.

Notes

CHAPTER TWO

1. Michel Foucault, *The Order of Things: An Archaeology of the Human Sciences*, New York: Vintage Books, 1994 (French original, 1966).

CHAPTER THREE

1. Walter Benjamin, 'Theses on the Philosophy of History' in *Illuminations*, edited and with an introduction by Hannah Arendt, trans. Harry Zohn, New York: Shocken Books, 1969, 253–64 (German original, 1955).
2. Alvin Toffler, *Future Shock*, New York: Bantam Books, 1970.

CHAPTER SIX

1. Émile Zola, *La Bête Humaine*, translated with an introduction and notes by Roger Pearson, Oxford: Oxford University Press, 1996 (French original, 1890).

CHAPTER SEVEN

1. Theodor Adorno and Max Horkheimer, *Dialectic of Enlightenment*, ed. Gunzelin Schmid Nerr, trans. Edmund Jephcott, Stanford, CA: Stanford University Press, 2002 (German original, 1947).
2. Friedrich von Schiller, *Letters on the Aesthetic Education of Man*, trans. Elizabeth M. Wilkinson and L.A. Willoughby, Oxford: Clarendon Press, 1967 (German original, 1795).

NOTES

CHAPTER EIGHT

1. Claude Lévi-Strauss, *Tristes Tropiques*, trans. John and Doreen Weightman, New York: Atheneum, 1974 (French original, 1955).
2. Claude Genoux, *Mémoires d'un enfant de la Savoie: les carnets d'un colporteur*, ed. Lucien Chavoutier, Montmélian: la Fontaine de Siloé, 2001.

CHAPTER NINE

1. Stéphane Courtois (ed.) *The Black Book of Communism: Crimes, Terror, Repression*, trans. Jonathan Murphy and Mark Kramer, Cambridge: Harvard University Press, 1999 (French original).
2. Author of *The Unknown Revolution*, 1917–1921, New York: Free Life Editions, 1974 (French original, 1947).

CHAPTER ELEVEN

1. Roberto Beningi's film was released in English as *Life Is Beautiful*.
2. Gérard Wajcman, "'Saint Paul' Godard contre 'Moïse' Lanzmann?", *Le Monde*, 3 December 1998.
3. A 1939 film by Jean Renoir, released in English as *The Rules of the Game* (1950).

CHAPTER TWELVE

1. Jean Baudrillard, *The Gulf War Did Not Take Place*, trans. Paul Patton, Bloomington, IN: Indiana University Press, 1995 (French original, 1991).

CHAPTER FIFTEEN

1. This title, *Bruit de fond*, comes from the French translation of the novel by Don DeLillo, *White Noise*, New York: Penguin, 2002.
2. Thierry de Duve, *Voici, 100 ans d'art contemporaine*, Paris: Ludion/ Flammarion, 2000.

CHAPTER SEVENTEEN

1. Jean-Jacques Delfour, '«Loft Story», une machine totalitaire', *Le Monde*, 19 May 2001.
2. 'Pouvoirs et stratégies', interview with Michel Foucault, *Les Révoltes logiques*, no. 4, winter 1977, p. 90.

CHAPTER EIGHTEEN

1. The film was first released in 2001, and was titled *The Lady and the Duke* in English.

CHAPTER TWENTY

1. Pierre Hadot, *La Philosophy comme manière de vivre*, interviews with Jeannie Carlier and Arnold I. Davidson, Paris: Albin Michel, 2001; Catherine Rambert, *Petite Philosophie du matin*, Paris: Le Grand Livre du mois, 2002; Roger-Pol Droit, *101 Experiments in the Philosophy of Everyday Life*, trans. Steven Romer, London: Faber & Faber, 2002; Michel Onfray, *Antimanuel de philosophie*, Paris: Bréal, 2001; Alain de Botton, *The Consolations of Philosophy*, Harmondsworth: Penguin, 2000.

CHAPTER TWENTY-THREE

1. The original French text is: *Je suis tombé par terre,*
   C'est la faute à Voltaire
   Le nez dans le ruisseau,
   C'est la faute à Rousseau !

CHAPTER TWENTY-FOUR

1. In question is the quarrel provoked by Daniel Lindenberg's work *Les Nouveaux Réactionnaires*.

CHAPTER TWENTY-SIX

1. Translator's note: This is my attempt at translating the well-known French song '*J'ai la mémoire qui flanche*' . . .
2. Robert Redeker, 'Les néopacifistes en guerre . . . contre la paix', *Le Monde*, 26 March 2003.

CHAPTER TWENTY-SEVEN

1. A still more striking illustration has since been provided by the case of Teri Schiavo, in which we saw the American Congress, in a full period of tax cuts and welfare system reform, sit as a matter of utmost urgency on a holiday weekend and vote in a law of exception to order the reconnection of an artificial feeding tube.

NOTES

CHAPTER TWENTY-NINE

1. Jean-Claude Milner, *Les Penchants criminels de l'Europe démocratique* [The Criminal Tendencies of Democratic Europe], Paris: Éditions Verdier, 2003.

CHAPTER THIRTY

1. Michel Foucault, *History of Sexuality, Volume 1: An Introduction*, trans. Robert Hurley, Harmondsworth: Penguin books, 1978 (French original, 1976).
2. David M. Halperin, *Saint Foucault: Toward a Gay Hagiography*, New York: Oxford University Press, 1995.
3. Michel Foucault, *The Essential Works of Michel Foucault 1954–84* (in 4 volumes), edited by Robert Hurley, James D. Faubion and Paul Rabinow, New York: The New Press, 2000–2006.
4. Michel Foucault, *The Use of Pleasure: The History of Sexuality, Volume 2*, trans. Robert Hurley, Harmondsworth: Penguin books, 1992 (French original, 1984) and *Care of the Self: The History of Sexuality, Volume 3*, trans. Robert Hurely, Harmondsworth: Penguin books, 1990 (French original, 1984).

CHAPTER THIRTY-TWO

1. Nicolas Bourriaud, *Esthétique relationnelle*, Dijon : Les Presses du réel, 1998.

Index